The Spirit of Japanese Poetry

The Spirit of Japanese Poetry

Yone Noguchi

MINT EDITIONS

The Spirit of Japanese Poetry was first published in 1914.

This edition published by Mint Editions 2021.

ISBN 9781513282503 | E-ISBN 9781513287522

Published by Mint Editions®

 MINT
EDITIONS

minteditionbooks.com

Publishing Director: Jennifer Newens
Design & Production: Rachel Lopez Metzger
Project Manager: Micaela Clark
Typesetting: Westchester Publishing Services

The Poet

Out of the deep and the dark,
A sparkling mystery, a shape,
Something perfect,
Comes like the stir of the day;
One whose breath is an odour,
Whose eyes show the road to stars,
The breeze on his face,
The glory of Heaven on his back.
He steps like a vision hung in air
Diffusing the passion of eternity;
His abode is the sunlight of morn,
The music of eve his speech;
In his sight
One shall turn from the dust of the grave
And move upward to the woodland.

—Yone Noguchi

CONTENTS

Editorial Note

The object of the Editors of this series is a very definite one. They desire above all things that, in their humble way, these books shall be the ambassadors of good-will and understanding between East and West—the old world of Thought and the new of Action. In this endeavour, and in their own sphere, they are but followers of the highest example in the land. They are confident that a deeper knowledge of the great ideals and lofty philosophy of Oriental thought may help to a revival of that true spirit of Charity which neither despises nor fears the nations of another creed and colour.

L. Cranmer-Byng
S. A. Kapadia

Introduction

There are beauties and characteristics of poetry of any country which cannot be plainly seen by those who are born with them; it is often a foreigner's privilege to see them and use them, without a moment's hesitation, to his best advantage as he conceives it. I have seen examples of it in the work of Western artists in adopting our Japanese traits of art, the traits which turned meaningless for us a long time ago, and whose beauties were lost in time's dust; but what a force and peculiarity of art Utamaro or Hiroshige, to believe the general supposition, inspired in Monet, Whistler and others! It may seem strange to think how the Japanese art of the Ukiyoye school, nearly dead, commonplace at its best, could work such a wonder when it was adopted by the Western hand; but after all that is not strange at all. And is it not the same case with poetry? Not only the English poetry, but any poetry of any country, is bound to become stale and stupid if it shuts itself up for too long a time; it must sooner or later be rejuvenated and enlivened with some new force. To shake off classicism, or to put it more abruptly, to forget everything of history or usage, often means to make a fresh start; such a start often begins being suggested by the poetry of some foreign country, and gains a strength and beauty. That is why even we Japanese, I dare say, can make some contribution to English poetry. The English poem, as it seems to me, is governed too greatly by old history and too-respectable prosody; just compare it with the English prose, which has made such a stride in the recent age, to see and be amazed at its unchanging gait. Perhaps it is my destitution of musical sense (a Western critic declared that Japanese are for the most part unmusical) to find myself more often unmoved by the English rhymes and metres; let me confess that, before perceiving the silver sound of a poet like Tennyson or Swinburne, born under the golden clime, my own Japanese mind already revolts and rebels against something in English poems or verses which, for lack of a proper expression, we might call physical or external. As my attention is never held by the harmony of language, I go straightforward to the writer's inner soul to speculate on it, and talk with it; briefly, I am sound-blind or tone-deaf—that is my honest confession. It is not only my own confession, but the general confession of nearly all Japanese; our Japanese minds always turn, let me dare say, to something imaginative.

It is my own opinion that the appearance of Basho, our beloved Hokku master, was the greatest happening of our Japanese annals; the Japanese poetry, which had been degenerating for centuries, received a sudden salvation through his own pain and imagination. His greatest hope, to become a poet without words, was finally realised; he was, as I once wrote on the Buddha priest in meditation:

> *"He feels a touch beyond word,*
> *He reads the silence's sigh,*
> *And prays before his own soul and destiny:*
> *He is a pseudonym of the universal Consciousness,*
> *A person lonesome from concentration."*

When the Japanese poetry joined its hand with the stage, we have the *No* drama, in which the characters sway in music, soft but vivid, as if a web in the air of perfume; we Japanese find our own joy and sorrow in it. Oh, what a tragedy and beauty in the *No* stage! I always think that it would be certainly a great thing if the *No* drama could be properly introduced into the West; the result would be no small protest against the Western stage, it would mean a real revelation for those people who are well tired of their own plays with a certain pantomimic spirit underneath.

We started our country as the land of poetry; our forefathers were poets themselves. They were free as the winds are free. When our modern young poets cry to go back to the age of their forefathers, they think that it is only the way to escape from the so-called literature and gain this poetical strength and beauty; it is their opinion that they find all the Western literary ideals in our Japanese ancient life and poetry. But I often quarrelled with them on the point that the real poetry of any country should be an expression of beauty and truth; we must build, I always insist, our poetry on our own true culture, which we formed through the pain and patience of centuries. It is my own opinion that the true Japanese poetry should be, as I once wrote, a potted tree of a thousand years' growth; our song should be a Japanese teahouse—four mats and a half in all—where we burn the rarest incense which rises to the sky; again our song should be an opal with six colours that shine within.

People who are already familiar with the Japanese poetry would ask me why I did not dwell on our *Uta* poetry at some length; I confess that my poetical taste desires far more intensity than the *Uta* poems, whose artificial execution often proves, in my opinion, to be their weakness rather than strength. Besides, they should be treated independently in a separate volume; they have their own poetical history of more than two thousand years.

"The Japanese *Hokku* Poetry" is the lecture delivered in the Hall of Magdalen College at the invitation of Mr. Robert Bridges, the Poet Laureate, and Dr. T. H. Warren, President of the College and Professor of Poetry in the University; and my lectures at the Japan Society, the Royal Asiatic Society, and the Quest Society have been based more or less on the other chapters in the book.

Y. N.
LONDON,
March 10*th*, 1914

I

The Spirit of Japanese Poetry

I come always to the conclusion that the English poets waste too much energy in "words, words, words," and make, doubtless with all good intentions, their inner meaning frustrate, at least less distinguished, simply from the reason that its full liberty to appear naked is denied. It is the poets more than the novelists who not only misinterpret their own meaning, but often deceive their own souls. When I say it seems that they take a so-called poetical licence, I mean that what they write about, to speak slangily, by the yard, is not Life or Voice itself; from such a view-point I do not hesitate to declare that the English poets, particularly the American poets, are far behind the novelists. I can prove with many instances that there are books and books of "poems" in which one cannot find any particular design of their authors; it is never too much to say that they have a good intention, though not wise at best; but, after all, to have only that good intention is not the way to make art or literature advance.

I always insist that the written poems, even when they are said to be good, are only the second best, as the very best poems are left unwritten or sung in silence. It is my opinion that the real test for poets is how far they resist their impulse to utterance, or, in another word, to the publication of their own work—not how much they have written, but how much they have destroyed. To live poetry is the main thing, and the question of the poems written or published is indeed secondary; from such a reason I regard our Basho Matsuwo, the seventeen-syllable *Hokku* poet of three hundred and fifty years ago, as great, while the work credited to his wonderful name could be printed in less than one hundred pages of any ordinary size. And it is from the same reason that I pay an equal reverence to Stephane Mallarmé, the so-called French symbolist, though I do not know the exact meaning of that term. While they are poets different in nature, true to say, as different as a Japanese from a Frenchman (or it might be said, as same as the French and the Japanese), it seems to me that they join hands unconditionally in the point of denying their hearts too free play, with the result of making poetry living and divine, not making merely "words, words, and words," and further in the point that both of them, the Japanese and the Frenchman, are poetical realists whose true realism is heightened or "enigmatised" by the strength of their own self-denial, to the very point that they have often been mistaken for mere idealists. Putting aside the question whether they are great or not, the fact that they have left little work behind is the point that I should like to emphasise; blessed be they who can sing in silence to the content of their hearts in love of perfection. The real prayer should be told in silence.

For a poet to have few lines in these prosaic days would be at least an achievement truly heroic; I think that the crusade of the Western poetry, if it is necessary, as I believe it is most momentous, should begin with the first act of leaving the "words" behind, or making them return to their original proper places. We have a little homely proverb—"The true heart will be protected by a god, even though it offer no prayer at all." I should like to apply it to poetry and say that poetry will take care of itself all by itself without any assistance from words, rhymes, and metres. I flatter myself that even Japan can do something towards the reformation or advancement of the Western poetry, not only spiritually, but also physically.

Japanese poetry, at least the old Japanese poetry, is different from Western poetry in the same way as silence is different from a voice, night from day; while avoiding the too close discussion of their relative merits, I can say that the latter always fails, naturally enough through being too active to properly value inaction, restfulness, or death; to speak shortly, the passive phase of Life and the World. It is fantastic to say that night and day, silence and voice, are all the same; let me admit that they are vastly different; it is their difference that makes them so interesting. The sensitiveness of our human nature makes us to be influenced by the night and silence, as well as by the day and voice; let me confess, however, that my suspicion of the Western poetic feeling dates from quite far back in the days of my old California life, when I was quite often laughed at for my aimless loitering under the moonbeams, and for my patient attention to the voice of the falling snow. One who lives, for instance, in Chicago or New York, can hardly know the real beauty of night and silence; it is my opinion that the Western character, particularly of Americans, would be sweetened, or at least toned down, if that part of the beauty of Nature might be emphasised. Oh, our Japanese life of dream and silence! The Japanese poetry is that of the moon, stars, and flowers, that of a bird and waterfall for the noisiest. If we do not sing so much of Life and the World it is not from the reason that we think their value negative, but from our thought that it would be better, in most cases, to leave them alone, and not to sing of them is the proof of our reverence toward them. Besides, to sing the stars and the flowers in Japan means to sing Life, since we human beings are not merely a part of Nature, but Nature itself. When our Japanese poetry is best, it is, let me say, a searchlight or flash of thought or passion cast on a moment of Life and Nature, which, by virtue of its intensity, leads us to the conception of the whole; it is swift, discontinuous, an isolated piece. So it is the best of our seventeen-syllable *Hokku* and thirty-one syllable *Uta* poems that by their art, as Tsurayuki remarks in his Kokinshiu preface "without an effort, heaven and earth are moved, and gods and demons invisible to our eyes are touched with sympathy"; the real value of the Japanese poems may be measured by what mood or illusion they inspire in the reader's mind.

It is not too much to say that an appreciative reader of poetry in Japan is not made, but born, just like a poet; as the Japanese poetry is never explanatory, one has everything before him on which to let his imagination freely play; as a result he will come to have an almost personal attachment to it as much as the author himself. When you realise that the expression or words always mislead you, often making themselves an obstacle to a mood or an illusion, it will be seen what a literary achievement it is when one can say a thing which passes well as real poetry in such a small compass mentioned before; to say "suggestive" is simple enough, the important question is how? Although I know it sounds rather arbitrary, I may say that such a result may be gained partly (remember, only partly) through determination in the rejection of inessentials from the phrase and the insistence upon economy of the inner thought; just at this moment, while I write this article, my mind is suddenly recalled to the word which my old California poet-friend used to exclaim: "Cut short, cut short, and again cut short!"

The other day I happened to read the work of Miss Lizette Wordworth Reese, whose sensitiveness, the sweetest of all femininity for any age or race, expressed in language of pearl-like simplicity, whether studied or not, makes me think of her as a Japanese poet among Americans. When I read "A White Lilac" from *A Quiet Road* (what a title with the sixteenth-century dreaminess) I was at once struck by her sensitiveness to odour; as a better specimen let me give you the following:

"Oh, gray and tender is the rain,
That drips, drips on the pane;
A hundred things come in at the door,
The scent of herbs, the thought of yore.

"I see the pool out in the grass,
A bit of broken glass;
The red flags running wet and straight,
Down to the little flapping gate.

"Lombardy poplars tall and three,
Across the road I see.
There is no loveliness so plain,
As a tall poplar in the rain.

"But oh, the hundred things and more
That come in at the door;
The smack of mint, old joy, old pain,
Caught in the gray and tender rain."

With all due respect, I thought afterwards what a pity to become an American poetess if she has to begin her poem with "Oh, gray and tender is the rain"—such a commonplace beginning. I declared bluntly that I, "as a Japanese poet," would sacrifice the first three stanzas to make the last sparkle fully and unique like a perfect diamond. Explanation is forbidden in the House of Poesy for Japanese, where, as in the Japanese tea-house of four mats and a half, the Abode of Imagination, only the hints tender and gray, like a ghost or Miss Reese's rain, are suffered to be dwelling. Although of this American poetess it is said that her rejection of inessentials is tho secret of her personality and style, it seems that that rejection is not sufficient for my Japanese mind. If I be blamed as unintelligible from too much rejection, I have only to say that the true poetry should be written only to one's own heart to record the pain or joy, like a soul's diary whose sweetness can be kept when it is hidden secretly, or like a real prayer for which only a few words uttered are enough. Here I am reminded of a particular *Hokku*, a rain-poem like Miss Reese's, by Buson Yosano of the eighteenth century:

> *"Of the* samidare *rain*
> *List to the Utsubo Bashira pipe!*
> *These ears of my old age!"*

Is it unbelievable to you when I tell you that such is a complete Japanese poem, even a good poem? The poem, as you see, in such a Lilliputian form of seventeen syllables in the original, carries my mind at once to the season's rain and the Utsubo Bashira, or Pipe of Emptying, that descends from the eaves (how like a Japanese poem with a singular distinction of inability to sing!), to which the poet Buson's world-wearied old ears awakened; you will see that the "hundred things and more that come in at the door" of his mind should be understood, although he does not say it. Indeed, you are the outsider of our Japanese poems if you cannot read immediately what they do not describe to you.

My Japanese opinion, shaped by hereditary impulse and education, was terribly shattered quite many years ago when Edwin Markham's *The Man with a Hoe* made a furore in the American Press. I exclaimed: "What! You say it is poetry? How is it possible?" It appeared to me to be a cry from the Socialist platform rather than a poem; I hope I do not offend the author if I say that it was the American journalist whose mind of curiosity always turns, to use a Japanese expression, to making billows rise from the ground. Putting aside many things, I think I can say that Mr. Markham's poem has an inexcusable error to the Japanese mind; that is its exaggeration, which, above all, we cannot stand in poetry, and even despise as very bad taste. Before Edwin Markham there was Whittier, who sent out editorial volleys under the guise of poetry; it is not too much to say, I dare think, that *An American Anthology* by Mr. Stedman, would look certainly better if it were reduced to one hundred pages from its eight hundred; we are bewildered to see so many poet-journalists perfectly jammed in the pages. One cannot act contrary to education; we are more or less the creation of tradition and circumstance. It was the strength of the old Western poets, particularly Americans, that they preached, theorised, and moralised, besides singing in their own days; but when I see that our Japanese poetry was never troubled by Buddhism or Confucianism, I am glad here to venture that the Western poet would be better off by parting from Christianity, social reform, and what not. I think it is time for them to live more of the passive side of Life and Nature, so as to make the meaning of the whole of them perfect and clear, to value the beauty of inaction so as to emphasise action, to think of Death so as to make Life more attractive, although I do not insist upon their conforming themselves, as we Japanese poets, with the stars, flowers, and winds.

We treat poetry, though it may sound too ambitious to the Western mind, from the point of its use of uselessness; it rises, through a mysterious way, to the height of its peculiar worth, where its uselessness turns, lo, to usefulness. When one knows that the things useless are the things most useful under different circumstances (to give one example, a little stone lazy by a stream, which becomes important when you happen to hear its sermon), he will see that the aspect of uselessness in poetry is to be doubly valued since its usefulness is always born from it like the day out of the bosom of night; you cannot call it, I trust, merely a Japanese freakishness or vagary if we appear to you in the matter of poetry to make much ado about nothing. I dare say we have our own attitude toward poetry. I have no quarrel with one who emphasises the immediate necessity of joining the hand of poetry and life; however, I wish to ask him the question what he means by the word life. It is my opinion that the larger part is builded upon the unreality by the strength of which the reality becomes intensified; when we sing of the beauty of night, that is to glorify, through the attitude of reverse, in the way of silence, the vigour and wonder of the day. Poetry should be meaningful; but there is no world like that of poetry, in which the word "meaning" so often baffles, bewilders, disappoints us. I have seen enough examples of poems which appealed to me as meaningful and impressed another as hopelessly meaningless.

I deem it one of the literary fortunes, a happy happening, but not an achievement, that till quite recently our Japanese poetry was never annoyed, fatigued, tormented by criticism; it was left perfectly at liberty to pursue its own free course and satisfy its old sweet will. The phenomenon that the literary part of criticism could find a congenial ground in Japan might make one venture to explain it from the point of our being whimsical, not philosophical; emotional, not intellectual. I have often thought that this mental lack might be attributed to the inconsistency of climate and sceneries, the general frailty and contradictions in our way of living. What I am thankful for is that it has never degenerated into mere literature; when the Western poetry is in the hand, so to say, of men of letters, the greatest danger will be found in the fact that they are often the prey of publication; it is true that the Western poets, minor or major, or what not, have had always the thought of printing from early date till to-day. I know that at least in Japan the best poetry was produced in the age when publication was most difficult; I dare say that the modern opening of the pages for poets in the press, and the easy publication of their work in independent books, both in the West and the East, would never be the right way for the real encouragement of poetry. I read somewhere that a certain distinguished European actress declared that the true salvation of the stage should start with the destruction of all the theatres in existence; I should like to say well-nigh the same thing in regard to the real revival of poetry. Let the poets forget for once and all about publication, and let them live in poetry as the true poets of old days used to live. Indeed, to live in poetry is first and last. When one talks on the union of poetry and life, I am sure that so it should be in action and practice, not only in print. I have seen so many poets who only live between the covers and die when the ink fades away.

I often open the pages of *Hokku* poems by Basho Matsuo and his life of fifty years. He gained moral strength from his complete rejection of worldly luxuries. He lived with and in poverty, to use the Japanese phrase, *seishin* or pure poverty, by whose blessing his single-minded devotion was well rewarded; of course it was the age when material poverty was not a particular inconvenience, as to-day. I read somewhere in his life that he declined in the course of his pilgrimage to accept three ryo (equivalent to seven or eight pounds in the present reckoning), the parting gift by his students, as he was afraid his mind would be disturbed by the thought that his sudden wealth might become an attraction for a thief; oh, what a difference from the modern poets who call for a better payment! He had one of his poetical students at Kaga, by the name of Hokushi, who sent him the following *Hokku* poem when his house was burned down:

> *"It has burned down:*
> *How serene the flowers in their falling!"*

The master Basho wrote to Hokushi, after speaking the words of condolence, that Kyorai and Joshi (his disciples), too, had been struck with admiration by the poem beginning "It has burned down," and he continued "There was in ancient time a poet who paid his own life as the price of a poem. I do not think that you will take your loss too much to heart when you get such a poem." When Basho said the above, I believe that his admiration for Hokushi was more on account of his attitude toward life's calamity than for the *Hokku* poem itself. Hokushi did not study poetry in vain, I should say, when his own mind could keep serene like the falling flowers, while seeing his house burn to ashes. That is the real poetry in action. With that action as a background, his poem, although it is slight in fact, bursts into a sudden light and dignity.

Indeed the main question is: what is the real poetry of action for which silence is the language? To say the real poet is a part of Nature does no justice, because he is able more often to understand Nature better through the very reason of his not being a part of Nature itself. It is his greatness to soar out of Nature and still not ever to forget her in one word, to make himself art itself. And how does he attain his own aim? Is it by the true conception of Taoism, the doctrine of Cosmic change or Mood of the Universe, of the Great Infinite or Transition? Or is it through the Zennism, of whose founder, Dharuma, I wrote once as follows?

> *"Thou lurest one into the presence of tree and hill;*
> *Thou blondest with the body of Nature old;*
> *List, Nature with the human shadow and song,*
> *With thee she seems so near and sure to me,*
> *I love and understand her more truly through thee;*
> *Oh magic of meditation, witchery of silence,—*
> *Language for which secret has no power!*
> *Oh vastness of the soul of night and death,*
> *Where time and pains cease to exist."*

The main concern is how to regulate and arrange Nature; before arranging and regulating Nature, you have to regulate and arrange your own life. The thoughts of life and death, let me say, do not approach me; let me live in the mighty serenity of the Eternal! By the virtue of death itself, life grows really meaningful; let us welcome death like great Rikiu who, being forced to harakiri by his master's suspicion, drank the "last tea of Rikiu" with his beloved disciples, and passed into the sweet Unknown with a smile and song on his face for the very turn of the page.

When I think on my ideal poet, I always think about our old Japanese tea-masters who were the true poets, as I said before, of the true action; it was their special art to select and simplify Nature, again to make her concentrate and emphasise herself according to their own thought and fancy. Let me tell you one story which impresses me still as quite a poetical revelation as when I heard it first.

Three or four tea-masters, the aestheticists of all aestheticists, headed by famous Rikiu, were once invited by Kwanpaku Hidetsugu, a feudal lord of the sixteenth century, to his early morning tea; the month was April, the day the twentieth, whose yearning mind was yet struggling to shake off the gray-haired winter's despotism. The dark breezes, like evil spirits who feared the approach of sunlight, were huddling around under the eaves of Hidetsugu's tea-house; within, there was no light. And the silence was complete; then it was found that its old rhythm ("Oh, what a melody!") was now and then broken, no, emphasised, by the silver voice of the boiling tea-kettle. No one among the guests ever spoke, as the human tongue was thought to be out of place. The host, Kwanpaku Hidetsugu, was slow to appear on the scene; what stepped in most informally, with no heralding, was the Ariake no Tsuki, the faint shadow of the falling moon at early dawn, who came a thousand miles, through the perplexity of a thousand leaves, just enough to light a little hanging by the tokonoma, the *shikishi* paper tablet on which the following *Uta* poem was written:

> *"Where a cuckoo a-singing swayed,*
> *I raised my face, alas, to see*
> *The Ariake no Tsuki only remaining."*

All the guests were taken at once with admiration of the poem and the art of the calligrapher, famous Teika, who wrote it, and then of the art of the host, this feudal lord, whose aesthetic mind was minute and most fastidious in creating a particular atmosphere; and they soon agreed, but in silence, that the tea-party was especially held to introduce the poem or the calligrapher's art to them. And I should like to know where is a sweeter, more beautiful way than that to introduce the poem or picture to others; again, I should like to know where is a more beautiful, sweeter way than that to see or read the picture or poem. Great is the art of those old tea-masters who were the real poets of action.

YONE NOGUCHI

There is the garden path called *roji*, so to say, the passage into self-illumination, leading from the without to the within, that is to say, the tea-house under the world-wearied grayness of age-unknown trees, by the solitary granite lanterns, solitary like a saint or a philosopher with the beacon light in heart; it is here that you have to forget the tumultuous seas of the world on which you must ride and play at moral equilibrium, and slowly enter into the teaism or the joy of aestheticism. Now I should like to know if our lives are not one long *roji* where, if you are wiser, you will attempt to create the effects or atmosphere of serenity or poetry by the mystery of silence. There are many great tea-masters who have left us words of suggestion how to beguile and lead our minds from the dusts and ruin of life into the real roji mood that is the blessing of shadowy dreams and mellow, sweet unconsciousness of soul's freedom; I agree at once with Rikiu who found his own secret in the following old song:

> *"I turned my face not to see*
> *Flowers or leaves;*
> *'Tis the autumn eve*
> *With the falling light:*
> *How solitary the cottage stands*
> *By the sea!"*

Oh, vastness of solitariness, blessing of silence! Let me, like that Rikiu, step into the sanctuary or idealism by the twilight of loneliness, the highest of all poetry!

This same Rikiu left us another story which pleases my mind greatly. Shoan, his son, was once told by his father to sweep or clean the garden path as Rikiu, the greatest aestheticist with the tea-bowl, doubtless expected some guest on that day; Shoan finished in due course his work of sweeping and washing the steppingstones with water. "Try again," Rikiu commanded when he had seen what he had done. Shoan again swept the ground and again washed the stones with water. Rikiu exclaimed again: "Try once more." His son, though he did not really understand what his father meant, obeyed, and once more swept the ground and once more washed the stepping-stones with water. "You stupid fool," Rikiu cried almost mad; "sweeping and watering are not true cleaning. I will show you what is to be done with the garden path." He shook the maple-trees to make the leaves fall, and decorate the ground with the gold brocade. "This is the real way of cleaning," Rikiu exclaimed in satisfaction. This little story always makes me pause and think. Indeed, the approach to the subject through the reverse side is more interesting, often the truest. Let me learn of death to truly live; let me be silent to truly sing.

II

THE JAPANESE HOKKU POETRY

Walter Pater, in one of his much-admired studies, *The School of Giorgione*, represents art as continually struggling after the law or principle of music, toward a condition which music alone completely realises; "lyrical poetry," he thinks, "approaches nearest to that condition, hence is the highest and most complete form of poetry; and," he adds, "the very perfection of such poetry often appears to depend, in part, on a certain suppression or vagueness of mere subjects, so that the meaning reaches us through ways not distinctly traceable by the understanding. . ."

I should like to develop Pater's literary ideal a little further through Lao Tze's canon of spiritual anarchism (it's nothing so strange to speak sometimes the names of this ancient Chinese sage and the modern English critic side by side); is it not that to mean nothing means all things; again, not to sing at all means to sing everything? Lao Tze says: "Assert non-assertion. Practise non-practice. Taste non-taste"; let me here add one more line: "Express in non-expression." To attach too closely to the subject matter in literary expression is never a way to complete the real saturation; the real infinite significance will only be accomplished at such a consummate moment when the end and means are least noticeable, and the subject and expression never fluctuate from each other, being in perfect collocation; it is the partial loss of the birthright of each that gains an artistic triumph. I have a word which is much used carelessly in the West, but whose true meaning is only seldom understood, that is the word of suggestion. I have an art; that is the art of suggestion. What suggestion? you might ask. I will point the way, if you are given a right sort of artistic susceptibility, where the sunlight falls on the laughter of woods and waters, where the birds sing by the flowers; again I will point, if you are able to read the space between the lines, to the pages of the Japanese seventeen-syllable *Hokku* poems, the tiniest poems of the world.

I do never mean that the *Hokku* poems are lyrical poetry in the general Western understanding; but the Japanese mind gets the effect before perceiving the fact of their brevity, its sensibility resounding to their single note, as if the calm bosom of river water to the song of a bird. One of the

English critics exclaims from his enthusiasm over *Hokku*: "That is valuable as a talisman rather than as a picture. It is a pearl to be dissolved in the wine of a mood. Pearls are not wine, nor in themselves to be thought of as a drink, but there is a kind of magic in the wine in which they are dissolved." That magic of the *Hokku* poems is the real essence of lyrical poetry even of the highest order. I do not see why we cannot call them musical when we call the single note of a bird musical; indeed, they attain to a condition, as Pater remarked, which music alone completely realises, because what they aim at and practise is the evocation of mood or psychological intensity, not the physical explanation, and they are, as I once wrote:

> *"A creation of surprise (let me say so)*
> *Dancing gold on the wire of impulse."*

And even from the narrow scientific understanding of the term they are musical, as they are the first seventeen syllables out of the euphonic thirty-one-syllable *Uta* poem, whose birth, according to the mythological assumption, was in the same time when heaven and earth were created; a reader who knows no Japanese will find his ears softened, to take one at random, on hearing the following *Hokku* poem:

> *"Osoki hi no*
> *Tsumorite toki*
> *Mukashi kana."*

Or again in the following by the same author, Buson Yosano (1716–1783):

> *"Kindachi ni*
> *Kitsune bake tari*
> *Yoi no Haru."*[1]

1.
> *"Kindachi ni*
> *Kitsune bake tari*
> *Yoi no Haru."*

Prince young, gallant, a masquerading fox goes this spring eve.

You must have seen somewhere a humorous Japanese sketch in which a fantastic young prince wearing a hunting dress of potato leaves (why, he is a masquerading fox; see his tail, which assumes the place of a back-sword), and having his hair dressed with

Such brevity of poetical form might be well compared with an eight-coloured butterfly or a white dew upon summer grasses; again, with a tiny star carrying the whole large sky at its back. When I say that the *Hokku* poet's chief aim is to impress the readers with the high atmosphere in which he is living, I mean that the readers also should be those living in an equally high poetical atmosphere; such readers' minds will certainly respond to the wistfulness and delicacy of the *Hokku*, a wistfulness and delicacy not to be met with in the general run of English poetry.

I admit that they will appear first, at once, to you to be the vagrant utterances of a primitive man who, uneducated, sings of whatever his fancy or whim finds fair and striking. But I should like to ask what poet is not primitive in heart when he is true. The real poet in the Japanese understanding is primitive, as primitive are the moon and flowers; the voice of a wind we hear to-day is the same voice which echoed, let me say, to the ears of Adam and Eve through the valley and trees. I think it is quite a happy epithet to call the poets the friends of winds and moon. You may think it a pantheism if you will, when our Japanese poets go to Nature to make life more meaningful, sing of flowers and birds to make humanity more intensive; it was from the sense of mystical affinity between the life of Nature and the life of man, between the beauty of flowers and the beauty of love, that I wrote as follows:

> *"It's accident to exist as a flower or a poet;*
> *A mere twist of evolution but from the same force:*
> *I see no form in them but only beauty in evidence;*
> *It's the single touch of their imagination to get the embodiment of a*
> *poet or a flower:*
> *To be a poet is to be a flower,*
> *To be the dancer is to make the singer sing."*

Basho, the most famous *Hokku* poet of the seventeenth century, in fact, the real creator of the seventeen-syllable form of poetry, spent the best part of his life of fifty years in travelling; travelling, or to use a better

---

two or three wheat-straws after an old fashion, is lightly drawn under the new moon of a spring eve; the evening in Japan's April or May, rich, misty, perhaps at Kyoto, has such charm to make the mind of a fox beautifully unbalanced. Buson's love of an irresistibly pretty gesticulation of life and nature lets him excel in such a subject as a spring night, whose soul is that of poetry.

word, pilgrimage, for this Basho ("Basho" is his *nom de plume*, meaning banana-leaves whose flexibility against winds and autumn, he imagined, was that of his ephemeral life) was never searching after life's selfish joy; it was a holy service itself, as if a prayer-making under the silence of a temple; is there a more holy temple than the bosom of Nature? He travelled East and West, again South and North, for the true realisation of the affinity of life and Nature, the sacred identification of himself with the trees and flowers; he could not forget Nature even at the final death moment when he wrote a *Hokku* poem saying:

> *"Lying ill on journey,*
> *Ah, my dreams*
> *Run about the ruin of fields."*

The thought of Basho makes me think of Walt Whitman; the above poem of Basho's recalls to my mind Whitman's pathos of his last years: "I am an open-air man: winged. I am an open-water man: aquatic. I want to get out, fly, swim I am eager for feet again. But my feet are eternally gone." I read somewhere of Whitman denying the so-called "literature" (accidentally laughing, scorning, jeering at his contemporaries). "I feel about literature what Grant did about war. He hated war. I hate literature. I am not a literary West Pointer; I do not love a literary man as a literary man, as a minister of a pulpit loves other ministers because they are ministers: it is a means to an end, that is all there is to it: I never attribute any other significance to it." Basho always spoke from the same reason that there was no other poetry except the poetry of the heart; he never thought literature or so-called literature to be connected with his own poetry, because it was a single noted adoration or exclamation offhand at the almost dangerous moment when his love of Nature suddenly turned to hatred from the too great excess of his love. It is the word of exclamation; its brevity is strength of his love. *Hokku* means literally a single utterance or the utterance of a single verse; that utterance should be like a "moth light playing on reality's dusk," or "an art hung, as a web, in the air of perfume," swinging soft in music of a moment. Now again to return to Whitman. He remarks somewhere: "New York gives the literary man a touch of sorrow; he is never quite the same human being after New York has really set in; the best fellows have few chances of escape." Although Basho never expressed his hatred of city life in such a bold emphasis of words as Whitman, as his were the days when politeness of language was inculcated, the fact of his spending the greater part of his life, now on the sleepy back of a horse by a whispering stream, then seeing the fallen petals in deep sigh with country rustics, is proof enough that he regarded a city life as fatal to his poetry; he was, with Whitman, a good exemplar to teach us how to escape the burden of life; and again the *Hokku* poems, if intelligently translated into English (indeed that is an almost impossible literary feat to accomplish), will give the most interesting example to encourage the modern literary ideal of the West which seeks its salvation in escape from the so-called literary.

My literary mind of *Hokku* love often finds itself highly pleased, as if when a somewhat familiar face is disclosed out of the crowd under a strange flash of light, to discover a *Hokku* touch in English poetry in my casual reading of my beloved poet's pages; I will call Landor a *Hokku* poet when he wrote the following:

> *"I warmed both hands before the fire of life;*
> *It sinks, and I am ready to depart."*

This poetical atmosphere is the atmosphere in which Buson wrote, as I mentioned before,

> *"Osoki hi no*
> *Tsumorite toki*
> *Mukashi kana."*

which might be translated as follows:

> *"Slow-passing days*
> *Gathered, gathering,—*
> *Alas, past far-away, distant!"*

Although the poet simply appears to recollect the past (making objectivity in poetical expression reveal his subjectivity clearer through the virtue of the poem's being a good *Hokku*), the meaning that he is ready to depart when fate calls upon him will be well understood by those whose spiritual endowment is rich enough to read the part of silence. I can point out sometimes a *Hokku* effect of poetry even from the works of Tennyson and Browning; it is not too much to say that many of Wordsworth's poems could be successfully turned as series of *Hokku* poems. My humanity always thrills, trembles in reading "The Toys," from Coventry Patmore's *The Unknown Eros*, as if, when I read Chiyo's lamentation over her dead boy, a little thing really worthy of a place in any Greek Anthology:

> *"The hunter of dragonflies,*
> *To-day, how far away*
> *May he have gone!"*

Now let me contrast one of the well-known poems by Rossetti, "The Woodspurge," with a *Hokku* poem by Basho. "In moments of intense sorrow or grief," Lafcadio Hearn was wont to repeat in his class-room, "when all the energies are paralysed, all the mental faculties being stricken into inaction, any new or strange thing, however small, seen accidentally, will be remembered for all the rest of one's life." Rossetti has the following:

> *"From perfect grief there need not be*
> *Wisdom or even memory:*
> *One thing then learnt remains to me,*
> *The woodspurge has a cup of three."*

And Basho's poem to which I invite your attention has the following:

> *"Being tired,—*
> *Ah, the time I fall into the inn,—*
> *The wistaria flowers."*

Our Japanese *Hokku* master, the lone poet on a certain forgotten highway, found the beauty of the wistaria flowers most strikingly appealing to his poetic mind now simplified, therefore intensified, through the physical lassitude resulting from the whole day's walk; if Basho had been a man of more specialised mind, in the modern sense, he might have taken notice of some forgotten flower with its peculiarity by his feet, when he rested himself on the bamboo porch of a country inn, perhaps facing the open garden where the evening silence already had begun to steal.

When I say the best *Hokku* poems do never know their own limitations, (remember, they are only seventeen syllables), that is because they are of the most essential of all the essential languages, which is inwardly extensive and outwardly vague; a severe restraint imposed on one side will be well balanced by the large freedom on the other. As in any poem of any other country, the Japanese poet's work also rests on the belief that poetry should express truth in its own way; by that truth we Japanese mean Nature; again by that Nature the order of spontaneity. Lao Tze says: "Man takes his law from the earth; the Earth its law from Heaven; Heaven its law from *Tao*; but the law of *Tao* in its own spontaneity." It was the Chinese sage's greatness to interpret, you might say, psychologically God by the single word of spontaneity. When I measure our Japanese poetical truth by the said spontaneity, my mind dwells on the best *Hokku* poems as the songs "with no word, not tyrannised by form," on which I wrote as follows:

"A birth of genius,
Ascension of creative life,
Passion indefinable,
Accident inevitable:

A song, thou art phenomenon but not achievement."

They are the voice of spontaneity which makes an unexpected assault upon Poetry's summit; the best expression for it would be, of course, suggestion or hint of its eccentricity or emphasis. As the so-called literary expression is a secondary matter in the realm of poetry, there is no strict boundary between the domains generally called subjective and objective; while some *Hokku* poems appear to be objective, those poems are again by turns quite subjective through the great virtue of the writers having the fullest identification with the matter written on. You might call such collation poetical trespassing; but it is the very point whence the Japanese poetry gains unusual freedom; that freedom makes us join at once with the soul of Nature. I admit that when such poetical method is carried to the extreme, there will result unintelligibility; but poetical unintelligibility is certainly better than the imbecility or vulgarity of which examples abound, permit me to say, in English poetry. It is the aim of this Japanese poetry that each line of the poem should appeal to the reader's consciousness, perhaps with the unconnected words, touching and again kindling on the particular association; there is ample reason to say that our poetry is really searching for a far more elusive effect than the general English poetry.

As I said before, the *Hokku* poems are, unlike the majority of English poems, the expression of the moods or forces of the writer's poetical exertion, and their aim, if aim they have, is hardly connected with the thing or matter actually stated, but it casts a light on the poetical position in which the writer stands; although the phrase might be taken wrongly in the West, our Japanese poets at their best, as in the case of some work of William Blake, are the poets of attitude who depend so much on the intelligent sympathy of their readers. Their work is like a silent bell of a Buddhist temple; it may not mean anything for some people, like that bell which has no voice at all. But the bell rings out, list, in golden voice, when there is a person who strikes it; and what voice the bell should have will depend on the other. And again the *Hokku* poem is a bell helpless, silent, when with no reader to cooperate; when I say that the readers of Japanese poetry, particularly this *Hokku* poem, should be born like a poet, I count, I should say, their personal interest almost as much as that of the writers themselves. Therefore in our poetry the readers assume an equally responsible place; and they can become, if they like, creators of poems which in fact are not their own work, just as if one with a bell-hammer did create the bell in the real sense. We have one very famous Hokku in the following:

"Furu ike ya
Kawazu tobikomu
Mizu no oto."

("The old pond!
A frog leapt into—
List, the water sound!")

I should like, to begin with, to ask the Western readers what impression they would ever have from their reading of the above; I will never be surprised if it may sound to them to be merely a musician's alphabet; besides, the thought of a frog is even absurd for a poetical subject. But when the Japanese mind turns it into high poetry (it is said that Basho the author instantly awoke to a knowledge of the true road his own poetry should tread with this frog poem; it has been regarded in some quarters as a thing almost sacred although its dignity is a little fallen of late), it is because it draws at once a picture of an autumnal desolation reigning on an ancient temple pond whose world-old silence is now broken by a leaping frog. But a mind of philosophical turn, not merely a lover of description, would please to interpret it through the so-called mysticism of the Zen sect Buddhism. Basho is supposed to awaken into enlightenment now when he heard the voice bursting out of voicelessness, and the conception that life and death were mere change of condition was deepened into faith. It is true to say that nobody but the author himself will ever know the real meaning of the poem; which is the reason I say that each reader can become a creator of the poem by his own understanding as if he had written it himself.

Take the following poem by Buson:

"*Katamari ni*
Muchiutsu
Ume no aruji kana."

(*"The lump of clay*
He beats with a stick,—
He, the master of the plum-orchard.")

There might be many people, I believe, who will wonder where in the world poetry will come in from a piece of clay beaten by a stick. But be patient, my friends. This is quite an excellent *Hokku* poem; here we have a scene of some old retired master of a plum-orchard now in a stroll ("And day's at the morn; morning's at seven," perhaps as in Robert Browning's song in *Pippa Passes*), who beats a lump of clay playfully while walking lazily. And go again to the lines of great Browning:

"*God's in His Heaven—*
All's right with the world."

Do you still call the above *Hokku* nonsense? Take one more poem by Buson in the following:

"*Suzushisa ya*
Kanewo hanaruru
Kaneno koye."

(*"Oh, how cool—*
The sound of the bell
That leaves the bell itself.")

Some little amplification would perhaps help in understanding the beauty of the above poem; but if your sensitive ears can differentiate the sounds of a bell in the daytime and during the night it is certainly futile to dwell on it. Although the author never tells when he heard the bell, I would understand it to be the bell of very early Summer morning, when the whole world and life are in perfect silence; if you awake at such an hour, your bodily composure making your ears doubly susceptible to any sound, I am sure your mind will become at once cooler with the sound of a bell which, with the finest feeling, leaves the wooden bell-hammer, and bids good-bye. And take still one more poem by the same author in the following:

> *"Haru no voya*
> *Yoi akebono no*
> *Sono Nakani."*

> *("The night of the Spring,—*
> *Oh, between the eve*
> *And the dawn.")*

The old Chinese poets sang on the Spring eve, prizing it above many thousand pounds in gold, while the Japanese *Uta* poets of ancient days admired the purple-coloured dawn of Spring; in the opening passages of Sei Shonagon's *Makura Zoshi* or *Pillow Sketches* we have the following: "In Spring," to use Aston's translation, "I love to watch the dawn grow gradually white and whiter, till a faint rosy tinge crowns the mountain's crest, while slender streaks of purple cloud extend themselves above." Such is the beauty of a Spring dawn. Now Buson is pleased to introduce the night of the Spring which should be beautiful without questioning, since it lies between those two beautiful things, the eve and the dawn; and we are thrice glad with this Buson's *Hokku*.

I have quite an interest in the pages of English translation or free rendering of our Japanese poetry, because I learn from them the point of the Western choice of the subjects, and where the strength or weakness of the English mind lies in poetical writing; take the following *Hokku* poem with the translation by Edwin Arnold and Miss Walsh:

> *"Asagawo ni*
> *Tsurube torarete*
> *Morai mizu."*

("The morning-glory
Her leaves and bells has bound
My bucket handle round.
I could not break the bands
Of these soft hands.
The bucket and the well to her left,
'Let me some water, for I come bereft.'")

("All round the rope a morning glory clings;
How can I break its beauty's dainty spell?
I beg for water from a neighbour's well.")

With due respect to these translators, I ask myself why the English mind must spend so much ink while we Japanese are well satisfied with the following:

"The well-bucket taken away
By the morning-glory—
Alas, water to beg!"

Is it not the exact case as when the Western fountain-pen attempts to copy a Japanese picture drawn with bamboo brush and incensed Indian ink on a rice paper, in which formlessness, like that of a summer cloud, is often a passport into the sky of the higher art of Japan? When the English poet must cling to such an exactitude, let me dare say, as if a tired swimmer with a life-belt, I have only to wonder at the general difference between East and West in the matter of poetry. Take another example to show in what direction the English poetical mind pleases to turn:

"I thought I saw the fallen leaves
Returning to their branches:
Alas, butterflies were they."

What real poetry is in the above, I wonder, except a pretty, certainly not high ordered, fancy of a vignettist; it might pass as fitting specimen if we understand *Hokku* poems, as some Western students delight to understand *Hokku* poems, by the word "epigram." Although my understanding of that word is not necessarily limited to the thought of pointed saying, I may not be much mistaken to compare the word with a still almost dead pond where thought or fancy, nay the water, hardly changes or procreates itself; the real *Hokku*, at least in my mind, are a running living water of poetry where you can reflect yourself to find your own identification. (Therefore the best *Hokku* poem is least translatable in English or perhaps in any language.) It is, as I wrote already somewhere, "like a dew upon lotus-leaves of green, or under maple-leaves of red, which, though it is nothing but a trifling drop of water, shines, glitters, and sparkles now pearl-white, then amethyst-blue, again ruby-red, according to the time of day and situation; better still to say this *Hokku* is like a spider-thread laden with the white summer dews, swaying among the branches of a tree like an often invisible ghost in the air, on the perfect balance; that sway indeed, not the thread itself, is the beauty of our seventeen-syllable poem."

But you must know that such language can only apply to the very best *Hokku*, which, when introduced with sympathy rather than mere intelligence, will serve, through their magic of potential speech, using Arthur Ransome's phrase, or, let me say, potential effect, the modern Western writers or poets, as I said before, in search of an escape from the so-called literature; and these very best *Hokku* poems cannot be, in my opinion, more than half a thousand, nay, perhaps not more than two hundred and fifty in number from all works written in the last three hundred years. As there are indeed a most prodigious number of productions, my estimate will show, I believe, that even a dozen good *Hokkus* in one's whole life would not be regarded as a bad crop. In fact, the *Hokku* poems produced in the time before great Basho's appearance (1644–1694), when, under the influence of Teitoku, Teishitsu, and Soin Nishiyama, the school of art for art's sake, from the point of intricacy, mannerism, and affectation, was finally formed under the name of Danrin or "Forest of Consultation," are certainly not better than the butterfly poem quoted above; although Basho and his disciples (it is said that this Basho had three thousand disciples or followers in his life's days) rescued poetry from the hands of such a school of artistic vulgarity, the Shofu or "The School of Righteous Wind" which he established, we might say, with the power of faith and prayer, became soon again sadly degenerated; and it was Buson Yosano, who, now putting aside the brush for the picture, as he was an eminent artist of his own days, cried out for the so-called poetical revival of the Tenmei period. There was no more popular poetry once than this *Hokku* form, and still popular it is even to-day, when our insularity, poetical or otherwise, has been irrevocably broken. It goes without saying that where was a great master was a great *Hokku* poem which never makes us notice its limitation of form, but rather impresses us by the freedom through mystery of its chosen language as if a sea-crossing wind blown in from a little window. There have been, since the Grand Restoration, a few bold attempts at a *Hokku* revival, notably that of the late Shiki Masaoka; but it is not my present aim to follow after their historical record. What I hope to do at this moment is to point out to you the very value of the Japanese poetry of this peculiar form.

Arthur Ransome says somewhere in his paper called "Kinetic and Potential Speech": "It is like a butterfly that has visited flowers and scatters their scent in its flight. The scent and the fluttering of its bloom-laden wings are more important than the direction or speed of its flying." Such language applies to the *Hokku* poems at their best. I agree with Ransome in saying: "Poetry is made by a combination of kinetic with potential speech. Eliminate either, and the result is no longer poetry." But you must know that the part of kinetic speech is left quite unwritten in the *Hokku* poems, and that kinetic language in your mind should combine its force with the potential speech of the poem itself, and make the whole thing at once complete. Indeed, it is the readers who make the *Hokku*'s imperfection a perfection of art.

III

No: The Japanese Play of Silence

I

THE WORD DIGNITY, APPLIED TO the dramatic art, may mystify you, though it may not necessarily mislead you, because it is often mistaken for the pessimism which is apology at best. In emphasising the independence of the Japanese No drama, I have in mind the special audience it created with the patience of centuries. When I say that it has no need to wait on its audience, I have in my mind the fact that it was that very audience which originated and perfected it as we see it to-day on the stage of Kanze, or Hosho, or Umewaka, or Yamashina, or Kudan, of Tokyo. It is not too much to say that the audience, not more than three hundred in number for each performance—is that not a large enough audience?—are all of them *No* actors themselves. It is beautiful to see them, like fully flowed water blessed by sunlight, in the appreciation which is realised through silence, its highest reach seen in their motionlessness of posture. It is true, though it may sound arbitrary to say it, that the real actors on the stage–not more than three in one play, as it is the simplest affair, this *No* (is that not enough characters, again I ask, to make poetry move?)–find their secret of fire or passion where the audience lose themselves. This *No* house is a sacred hall dedicated to poetry and song, where the actors and audience go straight into the heart of prayer in creating the most intense atmosphere of grayness, the most suggestive colour in all Japanese art, which is the twilight soared out of time and place; it is a divine sanctuary where the vexation of the outer world and the realism of modern life leave to follow, when on the stage, the eight persons of the chorus in two rows, with profile to the audience, and the musicians, a flute and two tambourines, with their backs to the wooden end wall at the back of the stage, take their own proper places, and the flute sends out, as the beginning of the performance, the thrill of invocation ages old, as if a cicada whose ghost-voice curses the present Japanese "civilisation." It is an oasis in the human desert of modern life, this little hall of the No play, where I often spend the whole day, as the performance begins usually as early as nine o'clock in the morning, and gain the thought that artistic Japan is not wholly lost; and I feel there happiness and sorrow rhythmically commingled, a human feeling already joined with deathlessness, seeing right before me the great ghost of the Past and Eternity, because the Present slips away like a mouse chased by sunlight.

You know well enough there is a great deal of cant in the term "appreciative audience" of modern usage in theatrical reviews or papers. When we must spend two or three years in realising how many others fail in becoming *No* appreciators, it means that those elected in this particular art, where appreciation is not less, perhaps is greater, than the acting itself, will find their own lives vitalised with the sense of power in Japanese weariness. When we feel the beauty of the monotony of the *No* drama that is gained by the sacrifice of variety, I think that our work of appreciation is just started. I cannot forget the impression carved on my mind, which was then roughened, stiffened, by the toss of Western life of quite many years, when I first entered Hosho's *No* house some ten years ago. It was the month of October, with maple-leaves and passion-flowers fallen, with birds and love flung away, whose gray heart was in perfect accord with this *No* performance. I smiled to my friend, who was a great appreciator, playfully but none the less delightedly, when I noticed the "honourable names" of those occupants, lords or barons or what not, written on the wooden tablets stuck on each box. I think I must have felt even uncomfortable on seeing myself among the select few. My plebeian mind, which was familiar with the general theatre-goers of other common houses created by advertisements, was struck by the sight of the dresses in quieter shade of the lady audience, even those of the younger ladies who put aside their wild whims to satisfy and not to break the quiet atmosphere of the *No* house; and I was surprised at the general quietude that overflowed from the hearts of artistic sensibility. The audience make me think of the people in the tea-room or *Sukiya* for a ceremonial sip of tea, wrapped in silence and grayness; what difference is there between the three hundred people in the hall, and the five persons that are the usual number to be put in the tea-room, since the theory of the non-existence of space to the enlightened has much meaning? When I saw the people here in the hall move in and out of the boxes, without spoken words, like silent birds from twig to twig, with a slight bow that was beautiful, the web-like passways again reminded me of a *roji* or garden path connecting the portico where the guests wait, with the tea-room where, you have to break away from the dust and din of the world, to prepare yourself for the aesthetic enjoyment of the tea. Such a comparison, I admit, may sound too elaborate or even improbable. But the point I wish to make is that the passways of the *No* hall mean more than the pathways of the pits of common theatres. If you cannot connect them with the "garden path" I would be glad to suggest to you, as a tea-master might when you step through the twilight by the moss-covered granite lantern in the *roji*, to think for a while of the shadow of summer foliage, or the stretch of a sea, or the slow fall of the evening moon, even after you have entered your own box, and be ready to enter the artistic world created by your heart gray and cold, and then you have to open the book of the libretto on your knees as the others do, with the sight of the chorus taking their own seats on the stage.

There is no other stage like this *No* stage, so small, being twenty-five feet square at the largest, all opened except the wall facing to the audience, where the painted old pine-tree, as old as the world, as gray as poetry, looms as if a symbol of eternity out of the mist–(think of the play of Takasago, the hosts of pine-trees in the shapes of an old man and woman singing deathlessness and peace)–the long gallery or bridge on the same level connected with the stage on the right, along which the *No* actors move as spectres and make the performance complete, the passage of a beginning and ending, I might say Life and Death. When you see the roof, you will be impressed by the dignity of existence itself which the Western stage has not; but, as you can create the portion called *Kakoi* or enclosure for the temporary purpose of a tea-gathering by the device of screens, so you can build the *No* stage at any time in your Japanese house, three or four rooms being combined when the most obedient screens slip away. And it is your poetical imagination–thank Heaven, imagination is everything for this *No*–to perfectly fill in the utter lack of stage scenery and furniture; though there are many occasions, to be sure, when you might be doubtful of your power of imagination as to imagine the deep valley of Arashiyama of cherry-tree fame with a few paper-made cherry-blossom twigs, the big bell-tower with the paper-made bell hung from a shaking wooden frame, and, too extraordinary still, to fancy the ship, water, oars, of course, from a bamboo pole. I dare say, however, it will delight minds tired from the burden of the spectacular show in the West; indeed, the time may be already at hand, or at any rate quite near, when the Western stage will heed the lesson of Japanese simplicity, particularly of this *No* drama, whose archaism might give a divine hint how to sift the confusion and to rhyme beauty and life with emphasis. I believe you will be moved, as I have been moved, and again will be on future occasions, now to smile and then to cry with the actors wearing the self-same mask of painted wood–(you know that *No* is the mask play to speak directly, although that is not an exact translation)–which, marvellously enough, seems to differentiate the most delicate shades of human sensibility; we should thank our own imagination which turns the wood to a spirit more alive than you or I, when neither the actors nor the mask-carvers can satisfactorily express their secret. I know that the mask is made to reserve its feeling, and the actors wonderfully well protect themselves from falling into the bathos of the so-called realism through the virtue of poetry and prayer; and when I realise it is from the same old humanity that tears and smiles, brothers or sisters by blood relation, spring forth, their difference being only a little shade of colour, the mystery that the *No* hall performs on our human minds will be explained to a great measure. This is the house of fancy where those who can only find strength from the crudity of their five senses have no right to step in, but the silent worshippers of the Imperfect will congregate for the holy exercise of ritual of their imagination; it is not the whole truth to say that it is the *No*'s dignity to command you to believe in its representation, though you may incline to think otherwise, as for instance in the case where a *No* character of a lady, whose voice and posture are not different from a man's, is resented on the stage, but it is for your poetical mind flatly to object to seeing the superficial reality, and to surrender all criticisms for the sake of appreciation. Indeed, the actual expression of the *No* stage is ever so slight and ephemeral, like many other artistic expressions, the sighs of crickets or shivers of flowers; we have gained, as we behold it, great brevity at an almost astonishing cost of human energy. It goes without saying that the plays themselves are brief; and I have many reasons to be thankful that the stage has never been troubled with the dropping curtain from the beginning till to-day, because the curtain only serves, in my opinion, to bar the stage, to remind us always that we have to restrain ourselves and not come into too close communication with the actors. And what use is the *No* hall if you cannot drop the curtain in your imagination? although it may not be so often as in other theatres even at this *No* hall, you have sometimes to drop the curtain yourself before the play is finished.

I have had occasion before to associate the *No* hall with the tea-room where, through the fragrance of tea, the melody of the boiling kettle, and the curl of incense, you will slowly but surely enter the twilight land of the Unknowable; when you are told that both of them were practically formed, encouraged, and developed under the rule of the Ashikaga lords from the early fourteenth century down to the close of the sixteenth century, who attempted, and even succeeded in their attempt, to invigorate human lives with that simple lesson of simplicity, the comparison, I think, will not seem a mere spiritual speculation. And was there ever a time like to-day when the complex is replacing the homogeneous, when we need such a lesson in all the aspects of life? What variety and richness have we earned, I ask, from making the entire sacrifice of that simplicity? I am glad to say that the *No* drama has fully revived from the temporary oblivion of fifty years ago, and has two or three hundred appreciators at each performance; if we treat it as a case of protest, I would say that protest is the thing we need most to-day. Whenever we think of the *No* plays, our thanks are first turned to Yoshimitsu, the third great lord of the Ashikaga government, the mighty propagandist of the tea-ceremonies and the *No* drama; and we must not forget Yoshimasa, the eighth lord who almost completed the drama as we have it to-day. It was the greatness of Hideyoshi Toyotomi, the wonderful fighter of Japan, to leave his name associated with Soyeki or Rikyu, the greatest of all tea-masters, and also with the *No* actors. When we remember that the simplicity and archaism of the so-called tea-ceremony grew out of the purism of the Zen monastery or priest hall of meditation, it will be clear enough that the *No* drama must have an equal connection with Buddhism; in fact, there is no play among those three hundred plays in existence which has no appearance of a priest whose divine power of meditation or prayer invariably leads the ghost of a warrior or a lady, or a flower, or a tree into the blessing of Nirvana. To call the *No* the ghost play has no real meaning, any more than to call it a priest play; the main point is to tell the human tragedy rather than comedy of the old stories and legends seen through the Buddhistic flash of understanding, as most of the plays were written by priests or by those people most influenced by Buddhism, as was quite natural in those days. The names of the authors, alas, are forgotten, or they hid their own names by choice. Even when some of their names, Seami and Otoami for instance, are given, it is said by an authority that they are, in fact, only responsible for the music, the dance, and the general stage management. It was the time when nobody asked who wrote them, if the plays themselves were worthy. What a difference from this day of advertisement and personal ambition! When I say that these plays were born like a mystery from the national impulse and love of literature, I mean that they are not the creation of one time or one age; it is not far wrong to say that they wrote themselves, as if flowers or trees rising from the rich soil of tradition and Buddhistic faith. As literature, they are things apart from the aristocratic writing encouraged by the Kyoto court in the former age, being democratic in sentiment, though not in the style of the lines and phrases, which are in truth the noblest expression of poetry, and might be compared with the magnificent dresses of stiff brocade the actors wear as they move along to the deep cadence of music; there are no better examples of epic poetry in our Japanese literature than the *No* plays; it is not too much to say that there is not a phrase, an image, an incident too much or too little, not a false note of atmosphere or feeling; they are exquisite and deathless, these most proud, most living, most unwasted rhythms of human song and heart-cries.

II

THIS *No*, ALREADY STRONGLY ENCOURAGED by the said Hideyoshi (many new pieces were added, in his time, to the already large repertory, and alterations were made to those already in practice) had become the most important factor of the nation's life, when the time came down to the Tokugawa feudal age. To recite lines from the *No*, and to act on the stage if possible, was regarded to be one of a gentleman's accomplishments; the *No* play, in contrast to the common theatre, held the most noble, dignified place of entertainment. And so it is to-day. It was thought even sacred; it began to assume the most necessary rôle at a wedding ceremony. With the singing of a passage from "Takasago," it is believed your wedlock will be sealed. "Takasago," the happy play celebrating constancy, endurance, health and longevity, is represented by an old man and an old woman busy in the work of raking up the pine-needles under the pine-trees. The passage says: "True it is that these pine-trees shed not all their leaves; their verdure remains fresh for ages long; even among evergreen trees–the emblems of unchangeableness–exalted is their fame to the end of time–the fame of the two pine-trees that have grown old together." What are these two pine-trees? Who are the old man and woman? The ghosts of the trees are nothing, but the old man and woman singing the age of golden and happy life. Among some three hundred plays now in existence, there is no other like "The Robe of Feathers" that gracefully carries the delicate, statuesque beauty of composition and sentiment. It is the play of a fairy whose feather-robe was stolen by a fisherman at Mio's pine-clad shore, while she was bathing, and was finally given back upon her promise to dance. Not to go to extremes, even in sadness, is taught in Japan to be the height of cultured manners; here we have every Oriental beauty and lamentation in the song of this fairy who could not fly back to the sky:

> *"Vainly my glance doth seek the heavenly plain,*
> *Where rising vapours all the air enshroud,*
> *And veil the well-known paths from cloud to cloud."*

She promised that she would dance the dance that makes the Palace of the Moon turn round, and would leave her dance behind as a token to mortal men, if her robe were restored to her. However, the fisherman doubted lest she might return home to heaven without dancing at all; then the fairy said:

> *"Fie on thee! The pledge of mortals may be doubted, but*
> *in heavenly beings there is no falsehood."*

As I said, the *No* is the creation of the age when, by virtue of sutra or the Buddha's holy name, any straying ghosts or spirits in Hades were enabled to enter Nirvana; it is no wonder that most of the plays have to deal with those ghosts or Buddhism. That ghostliness appeals to the poetical thought and fancy even of the modern age, because it has no age. It is the essence of the Buddhistic belief, however fantastic, to stay poetical for ever. Although the *No*'s repertory does not change, our conception and understanding will be altered; it is thus that they can keep always fresh themselves. Here we have one play called "Yama Uba" or "Mountain Elf"; the author, undoubtedly a learned priest, attempts to express by the play that we are souls much troubled in a maze of transmigration, indeed, like the Mountain Elf, who, it is said, spends all the dark night circling round the mountain. That mountain is a symbol of life itself. The plot grows intense at the point where enters a famous dancer called Hyakuma Yama Uba, a woman who has earned such a name from her dancing of the Mountain Elf circling round the mountain. She has lost her way in Kagero no Yama, or the Hill of Shadow, in a pilgrimage toward Zenkoji, the Holy Buddhist Temple; and here she meets the real Elf or Yama Uba, with large star-like eyes and fearful snow-white hair, who demonstrates to her the way how she encircles the mountain, nay the mountain of Life. The play ends as may be expected of this *No* play; after making her prayer to the Elf, the dancer disappears over mountains and mountains, as her life's cloud of perplexity is now cleared away, and the dusts of transmigration are well swept. This little play would certainly make a splendid subject for a modern interpretation. For some long while my mind dwelt on it, wishing to write something. And also a play called "Morning-Glory" is interesting; the flower, in the play, cannot enter Nirvana on account of her short life of only one morning, and her jealousies that burn on seeing the other flowers who enjoy a longer life. However, her ghost will disappear with satisfaction when she listens to a sermon from the priest. I have written a dramatic fragment on the subject after my own fashion as follows:

The Morning-Glory

(A Dramatic Fragment)

PRIEST: "Who is the guide in Life's chartless field?

See the black robe of the priest for the changeless love of the
  Lord
(The robe is black, as black night, with mercy's depth):
I count my rosary, I count the sins of the world and life;
My prayer is the evening bell to turn them to rest.
My face is ever turned to joy and the West—
To the West, where lies Heaven, the only real place.
'Tis mine to make the suffering souls obedient to Law and
  Truth,
And then regain the song of dissolution and rest.
What is the flower that I see before my eyes?
Is it not the Morning-Glory, the flower of Summer's dream
  and dews?

It is strange to see it now when Autumn's silence
Has calmed down the fire and heart of Nature and song;
It is like a lyric forgotten and unsung–
Villager, tell me what flower it is."

VILLAGER: "Father, it is none other than the Morning-Glory."

PRIEST: "Is it the custom here to see it blooming under the pale
October sky?"

VILLAGER: "No, father. It is the first time I have seen it."

PRIEST: "See the tremor of the cup of the flower, as if it fears to
exist;

Oh, bareness of beauty that has soared out of life;
Is it a real morning-glory?
Is it not only imagination or pain itself?
I hear in its tremor a certain human speech, but voiceless.
What a mystery, what mournfulness, what tragic thrill!
I am a priest for whom stones and grasses prepare a nightly
bed,
A companion of water, trees, stars, and night;
Here will I sleep and solve the mystery with the power of
prayer.
Oh, flower, whatever name thou bearest, take me this night
as thy guest."

(*The villager goes out. It becomes dark; the first night-bell rings. The
priest recites the holy words. The lady enters as a waft of autumnal
wind.*)

LADY: "How my heart burns in madness and pain:

Oh, misery to be a prey to fire and unrest!
I am a wandering spirit of discontent from Hades,
After the Life that ascends, the Life of whiteness and the sun;
Oh, my hatred of dissolution and death!"

PRIEST: "Who art thou, lady? Thou seemest to be a soul dead,
but not dead,
Cursor of Nirvana, straying soul of unrest."

LADY: "Father, I am the spirit of the Morning-Glory."

PRIEST: "Dear child of dews and summer's impulse,
Why wanderest thou as a spirit of malice and evil?"

LADY: "I crave for the longer life of the many other flowers

That have only to grow with the sun and the day:
Oh, shortness of my life that ended before its day began!
How I long to feel the joy of life and the sun that was not mine!"

PRIEST: "Poor child, there is no life where is no death:

Death is nothing but the turn or change of note.
The shortest life is the sweetest, as is the shortest song:
How to die well means how to live well.
Life is no quest of longevity and days:
Where are the flowers a hundred years old?
Oh, live in death and Nirvana, live in dissolution and rest,
Make a life out of death and darkness;
Lady or flower, be content, be finished as a song that is sung!"

LADY: "Happy am I to hear such words, holy father,
Pray, pray for my sad soul that it may return to Hades and rest!"

PRIEST: *"Namu, amida butsu . . ."*

(*The lady disappears at once into the Morning-Glory. The moon rises. The flower withers. The midnight bell rings.*)

IV

THE EARLIEST JAPANESE POETRY

I

I USED TO LINGER AROUND the spot at Kamakura marked by a stone commemorating the street preaching of Nichiren, that undaunted spirit of a Buddhist priest born to a fisher's family in the Awa province in 1222, whose belief in the mysterious law of the White Lotus made him proclaim himself a prophet. And I would call to my imagination the continuous scene of persecutions the priest encountered gibes, railings, and even stones; he exclaimed at the beginning of the establishment of his own Buddhism, the sect of the White Lotus: "Know that all the sects in existence are a way to Hell, or the teaching of infernal hosts, or a heresy to destroy the nation, or an enemy of the land. These are not my words, but I found them in the sutra. And I am the messenger sent by the Worshipful for the teaching of the Real Law." When he attempted with the fervent tongue of a propagandist, to destroy at one stroke the old formulae and conceptions (or, more true to say, superstitions), by emphasising the individualistic fire of Buddhistic inspiration through whose activity he himself, as he declared, was the symbol of the infinite, his mind dwelt on the religious freedom born out of the idealism whose real manifestation can only appear through the highest development of the individual life. Nichiren saw clearly that Japan or Japanese life had been greatly harmed by the pessimistic interpretation of Buddhism, with its thought of Nirvana or peaceful haven far beyond where your absorption of the infinite can only be realised through the virtue of death, a death that does not recognise individuality. It was Nichiren's Activism (with apology to the German professor) to make life more meaningful, or again to make death more meaningful by that meaningful life, through the true Buddhism perfectly delivered from the despotism of ignorance or misconception; it is not far wrong to say that he alone found the meeting ground of Buddhism and the thoughts of our Japanese ancestors who, like sunflowers, most passionately sought after life and sunlight; on the sunflower I wrote once in *The Pilgrimage*, a book of verses, the following lines:

"Thou burstest from mood:
Marvel of thy every atom burning in life.
How fully thou livest!
Passionate lover of sunlight,
Symbol of youth and pride;
What absorption of thy life's memory,
Wonder of thy consciousness,
Mighty sense of thy existence!"

I am thankful to Nichiren, although his influence was not universal, for his hopeful, brighter mind (it was almost a Western mind), whose theological adventure would certainly please the followers of Eucken; it was the effect of the common pessimism of Buddhism or thought of Nirvana, combined with the morality and ethics of the Confucian literature, that our original Japanese mind, indeed quite a Celtic mind, like that of the young woman in Yeats' *Land of Heart's Desire*, who ever wearied of four tongues and wished to dance upon the mountains like a flame, had slowly but steadily lost its imagination and passion, and our lives had become hardened and disfigured. I leave aside the question of religion, because my chief concern for the present moment is in poetry whose rejuvenation may depend in some measure on a leader (such a leader as Nichiren in religion)–a leader who, like Whitman, will cry for "the splendid silent sun with all his beams full-dazzling" from the worshipping mind gladdened in Nature's sanctuary where our ancestors of three thousand years ago loved and lived. They had only the thought of life and birth, again the thought of birth and eternal life, never the thought of death and shadow; how our Japanese ancestors hated shadow and death is recorded in the first page of *Kojiki* or *Records of Ancient Matters*, the earliest book of Japanese literature in existence, as it was actually written or completed in A.D. 712. On this book I am going to dwell presently at greater length.

Go back to the age, that is many thousand years ago, when our Japanese mind was the Japanese mind pure and true, not the Japanese mind of later age, sometimes, doubtless, refined and polished, but always wounded and tormented by the despotic counsel of Chinese literature and Buddhism, therefore the Japanese mind like the sunflower, as I said before, a seeker of sunlight and life, the Japanese mind which is the personification of life's activity itself; you might call it the individualism, conscious or unconscious, following after the modern fashion. Let me exclaim as I exclaimed on the sunflower: "Marvel of thy every atom burning in life, how fully thou livest!" Our later Japanese spiritual history in literature or what not is more or less the history of quietism or negation in which the great charm and attraction is the thought of Cathay called death; I myself am pleased to sing on and of death because it makes life more strong, more beautiful, and more meaningful through its virtue of difference; and when I put stress upon the fusion of death with life, or upon valuing them equally, my mind thinks on the real spiritual freedom which will soon become a perfect idealism like a broader day born from the mixed souls of East and West. But when the Japanese mind of later days began to deal with death as a state lifeless, or something hard and final, then the thought of death ceased to have a better, greater influence on life; I despise such a death or such a thought of death. Go back to the age when our ancient Japanese did not know death and shadow, or even when they knew them, did not think much of them, or scorned them, like children laughing with winds and sun. To return to the age of *Kojiki* is indeed a rare treat in a time like to-day, when our aspiration or ambition, I mean that of the Japanese, only wastes its energy under incongruities, contradictions, and confusions of wild cross-currents of East and West.

II

HERE IN THE SECOND VOLUME of *Records of Ancient Matters* we have a story in Yamato-Take (not only that one story, but many other stories scattered in the first and last volumes) which will surely please a mind of Meredithian cast, epic-loving; one who fully endorses the so-called evolutional philosophy in the *Woods of Westermain*, or the cultivation of the power of the will, can find enough material for building his songs of tragic life; that rude philosophy of Meredith's our forefathers practised unconsciously. They such a self-strengthening mind and will (indeed the ancient Japanese thought was that life's greatest sin was the sin of weakness) as the old Norsemen thought; but our ancestors hailed, I believe, from a warmer climate with poetry and love; they were from the beginning poets and warriors. To return to Yamato-Take; he was a fierce type like Meredith's King Harold; while the English ballad ends with the following lines,

> *"Sudden, as it were a monster oak*
> *Split to yield a limb by stress of heat,*

> *Strained he, staggered, broke*
> *Doubled at their feet,"*

the story of Yamato-Take does not close with his death, because, from the hatred of death and shadow, his great dead spirit turned into a white bird eight fathoms long, soared up to the skies, and flew away over the seas, while the princesses and children who had shared equal pains under his conquering banner in the Eastern countries, pursued after that bird with their sad songs in heart, saying:

> *"Impeded are our loins in the plain,*
> *(The plain thick with bamboo-grasses):*
> *Oh! we are only on foot,*
> *Not flying through the skies."*

Again saying:

> *"Impeded are our loins as we go*
> *Through the seas, oh! tottering*
> *In the seas like herbs*
> *Grown in a great river-bed."*

This great valiant spirit, son of Emperor Keiko who was already afraid of his wonderful valour and ferocity, had been again sent away to conquer the unsubmissive bravoes of the East; on receiving the Imperial command, he said: "The Heavenly Sovereign must be thinking that I should die quickly, for after sending me to smite the wild people of the West, I am no sooner come up again to the capital than, without bestowing on me an army, he now sends me off afresh to subdue the wicked people of the East. So I think that he certainly thinks I shall die quickly." It was in the almost mythological ancient age when even the father, if he be weak, often happened to suffer the fate of a dove torn by a hawk; although Yamato-Take clearly knew his father's intention, he could not disobey his command, and beside, his love of fighting for fighting's sake made him start with renewed joy toward the East, where he began a series of successes with the slaying of the rulers of Sagama. He lost his beloved wife, Princess Oto-Tachibana, while crossing the sea of Hashiri Midzu, who drowned herself in the waves for the purpose of calming the storm by the sacrifice of her own self; it is said that the violent waves at once went down, and Yamato-Take's ship was able to proceed. His wife, this Japanese woman of many thousand years ago, already understood something of Meredith's following lines, of course with a variation of Japanese morality:

> *"The lesson writ in red since time first ran:*
> *A hunter hunting down the beast in man;*
> *That till the chasing but of its last vice,*
> *The flesh was fashioned but for sacrifice."*

Yamato-Take subdued and pacified all the East; now reaching the moor of Yagi on the way home, he suddenly felt weak and exclaimed: "Whereas my heart always felt like flying through the sky, my legs are now unable to walk; they have become rudder-shaped." Again at the village of Mike he exclaimed: "My legs are like threefold crooks, and very very weary."

Then he pulled his tired body to the Moor of Nobo, and from his deep love of his native land, he exclaimed, singing:

> *"O Yamato, the most hidden of lands,*
> *Yamato, snug within green hills,*
> *The hills encompassing thee with their fences,*
> *How delightful, O Yamato!"*

And then he passed away, singing:

> *"Thou whose life may be strong,*
> *Adorn thy hair, thou in health,*
> *With the bear-oak leaves from Heguri Mount,*
> *Be happy, my child!"*

Such was the last song of this great spirit; when you compare it with the Japanese songs of a later age, you will see that our ancestors, even at the moment of death, were never taken, to use the modern words, by the thought of pessimism or sentimentality; they were the singers of life and joy, not of death and tears.

They knew the world was never made for weak body and mind; they never exercised pity and compassion upon any form of weakness; they believed that the instant that one begins to doubt his own strength,

YONE NOGUCHI

whether it be of mind or body, all the hopes of winning life's prizes shall be at once overthrown. The fact that the sad destruction of life comes most surely through indulgence, not through struggle and pain, is well illustrated in the story of the Emperor Chuai somewhere in the second volume.

The book reads as follows: "So when the Heavenly Sovereign, dwelling at the Palace of Kashii in Tsukushi, was about to smite the land of Kumaso, the Heavenly Sovereign played on his lute; the Prime Minister, the noble Takeuchi, being in the pine court, requested the divine orders. Hereupon the Empress, divinely possessed, charged him with this instruction and counsel: 'There is a land to the Westward; in that land is abundance of treasures dazzling to the eye, from gold and silver downward. I will now bestow this land upon thee.' Then the Heavenly Sovereign replied saying: 'If one ascend to a high place and look Westward, no country is to be seen. There is only the great sea. What lying deities.' He pushed away his lute, playing no more, and sat silent. Then the deities became very angry, and said through the mouth of the Empress: 'Altogether as for this Empire, it is not a land over which thou oughtest to rule. Do thou go only the road to Hades!' The Prime Minister, the noble Takeuchi, said: 'I am filled with awe, my Heavenly Sovereign! Pray, continue playing thy great august lute.' The Heavenly Sovereign slowly drew his lute to him and languidly played on it. But when the sound almost immediately became inaudible, the Heavenly Sovereign was found, alas, dead." What a splendid subject this for a ballad or poem for a poet of Meredith's class.

The first note we encounter in opening the pages of this *Records of Ancient Matters* is our ancestors' conception of death as defilement; here we have a story of Izanami or His Augustness the Male-Who-Invites, who followed after his dead wife, Her Augustness the Female-Who-Invites, to the Land of Hades. When the male deity entreated her to come back again to the world, saying: "The lands that I and thou made are not yet finished making; pray come back!" Her Augustness the Female-Who-Invites was pleased to consent, but begged her husband to wait for a little while, as she had to discuss the matter with the deities of Hades. And she made him promise not to attempt to come to her while retiring within the palace of shadow. She tarried there so long, His Augustness the Male-Who-Invites would not wait any longer; so having taken and broken off, this mythology goes on to say, one of the end-teeth of this close-toothed comb stuck in the left bunch of his hair, he lit a light and went in and looked. Alas, his wife-deity was rotting with swarming maggots; in her head, it is written in the book, dwelt the Great Thunder, in her breast the Fire-Thunder, in her belly the Black Thunder, in her private parts the Cleaving Thunder, in her left hand the Young Thunder, in her right hand the Earth Thunder, in her left foot the Rumbling Thunder, in her right foot the Couchant Thunder, thus altogether eight Thunder Deities dwelt there. His Augustness the Male-Who-Invites, indeed, overawed at the sight, fell back, while his wife, who grew mad, exclaimed: "Thou hast put me to shame," and sent the eight Thunder Deities with a thousand and five hundred warriors of Hades to pursue him; but when they failed to meet him, Her Augustness the Female-Who-Invites came out herself in pursuit. She was blocked by a huge rock at the Even Pass of Hades which the male deity had placed there for his own protection; here these two deities stood opposite to one another, and Her Augustness the Female-Who-Invites was first to speak, and she said: "If thou doest like this, I will in one day strangle to death a thousand of the folk of thy land." Then His Augustness the Male-Who-Invites replied: "If thou doest this, I will in one day set up a thousand and five hundred parturition houses, and make the women bear children. Suppose a thousand people may each day die; but each day a thousand and five hundred people will be born." Thus birth conquered over death, the land of light over the land of shadow.

The great deity who defeated death and persuaded the deities of shadow not to pursue any more, said: "How hideous! I have come to a hideous polluted land; I will perform the purification of my person." Then he went into a plain and by a river near Tachibana in the island of Tsukushi, and began to purify and cleanse himself; it is written in the book, that, when he threw down his girdle, the Deity Road-Long Space was born thence, the Deity Master of Trouble from his upper garment he put aside, the Deity Master of the Open Mouth from his hat, and so on; thus the twelve deities altogether were born from his taking off the things that were on his person. And then from the bathing of his august person itself the other fourteen deities came into existence, among them the three illustrious children at whose birth His Augustness the Male-Who-Invites was rejoiced, the Heaven Shining Great August Deity from his left eye, His Augustness Moon-Night Possessor from his right eye, and His Brave Swift Impetuous Male Augustness from his nose. When these three deities, the first and second representing the sun and moon, the last ruling the seas, were born, we know that the creation of the world was in good shape. Not only from garment or eyes, but from anything or anywhere, indeed, even from a cough, our ancient deities, it was supposed, had such a power or magic to produce anything and everything by their free will, and they inspired their own personalities into the things they created. All the phenomena thus exhibited were, in our ancient Japanese mind, nothing but the symbol of life's active spirit; the great reverence of our forefathers toward the deities or gods was only fierce adoration or praising expression toward the power or strength which overflows from the bosoms of mighty personalities. I dare say that it would do justice to class it with the common pantheism or Nature-worship you find in ordinary barbarous tribes; when Japanese scholars like Motoori declare that the gods or deities of old Japanese mind were human beings, it is from their belief that the conception of gods should be based on the true realisation of life's fire.

Therefore, where was the real expression of life was a deity; there are no men who created so many gods or deities as the old Japanese; to them most impossible Japanese names were given, names like Ameno-Minaka-Nushi or Takami Musubi or Umashi-Ashikabi-Higoji.

III

THE DATE OF A.D. 712 WAS given to *Kojiki* (*Records of Ancient Matters*), in fact, the first written book in Japan, in its completion; it is said that Yasumaro, the author, took it all down from the lips of a certain Hiyedano Are, a Kataribe or reciter whose official function, at the very early Mikado's government of the Nara period, was to retell ancient records from his memory; it will be believed that they must have been changed, some parts perhaps omitted, or others added, during the process of retelling from one reciter to another. It is not my work to discuss here their value as legends of history; my important concern with them is their poetry, that is to say, the poetry of our Japanese ancestors, which runs through almost every page of the book. When I read love-songs diffused here and there in these three volumes it makes me think of a popular ditty like the following:

> *"What does never change,*
> *Since the days of the gods,*
> *Is the way how a river runs:*
> *What does never change*

Since the days of the gods,
Is the way how love flows."

One of the early love-songs is found when the Deity-of-Eight-Thousand-Spears went forth to woo the Princess of Nuna-Kaha and sang on his arrival at her house as follows:

"His Augustness the Deity-of-Eight-Thousand-Spears,
With no Spouse in the Land of the Eight Isles,
Now has heard in the far-off Koshi Land there is a maiden wise,
Now has heard there is a maiden beauteous:
Here he stands to truly woo her.
Here he goes backward and forward to woo her,
Having untied even the cord of his sword,
Having untied even his veil,
He pushes back the plank door shut by the maiden;
He stands here, forward he pulls it:
Here he stands, he soon hears the Nuge *singing on the*
green hill;
And the bird of the moor, the pheasant, resounds,
The bird of the yard, the cock, crows:
Oh, the pity that the birds should sing, oh, these birds!
Oh, how soon the night dawns!
Would that I could beat them to sickness and death!"

Then the Princess of Nuna-Kaha, without opening the door, sang from within:

"Thine Augustness the Deity-of-Eight-Thousand-Spears,
Being a maiden like a drooping plant,
My heart is just a bird on a bank by the shore;
My heart is now indeed a dotterel.
But it will soon become a gentle bird;
So as for thy life, do not deign to die."

Again she sang in the following fashion:

"The sun may hide behind the green hills,
The night, the jewel-black night will come forth;

I will then welcome thee.
Smile like the glad morning sun and come;

Thine arms white as rope of paper-mulberry bark,
Shall softly pat my breast soft as melting snow;
Patting each other interlaced,
Stretching out, pillowing us on each other's arms, on true
jewel-arms,
With outstretched legs, oh, will we sleep.
So speak not too lovingly,
Thine Augustness the Deity-of-Eight-Thousand-Spears!"

The Chief Empress, Her Augustness the Forward-Princess, got very jealous; His Augustness the Deity-of-Eight-Thousand Spears was greatly distressed when he was about to go from Izumo to the Land of Yamato; as he stood attired, with one hand on the saddle of his horse and one foot in his stirrup, he sang, saying:

"I take and carefully attire myself
In my garments black as the jewels of the moor;
Like the birds of the offing I look at my breast,
I find these are not good,
And cast them off on the waves of the beach.
I take and carefully attire myself
In my garments green as a kingfisher;
Like the birds of the offing, I look at my breast,
I find these too are not good,
And cast them off on the waves of the beach.
I take and carefully attire myself
In my raiment dyed in the sap of the dye-tree,
The pounded madder sought in the mountain
fields;
Like the birds of the offing, I look at my breast,
I find they are good.
My dear Younger sister, Thine Augustness!
Though thou say thou wilt not weep,
If, like the flocking birds, I flock and depart,
If, like the led birds, I am led away and depart,
Thou wilt hang down thy head

> *Like a single eulalia upon the mountain*
> *Thy weeping shall indeed rise*
> *As the mist of the morning shower,*
> *Thine Augustness, my spouse young like young herbs!"*

Then the Empress taking a great liquor cup, and drawing anear and offering it to her husband deity, sang as follows:

> *"Thine Augustness the Deity-of-Eight-Thousand-Spears!*
> *Thou, my Master-of-the Great-Land, being a man,*
> *Mayest have a wife young like young herbs,*
> *On all island headlands that thou seest,*
> *On every beach headland that thou lookest on;*
> *But as for me, alas, being a woman,*
> *I have no man except thee, I have no spouse except thee,*
> *Beneath the fluttering of the ornamented fence,*
> *Beneath the rustling cloth coverlet,*
> *Thine arms white as rope of paper-mulberry bark*
> *Softly patting my breast soft as melting snow,*
> *Patting each other interlaced,*
> *Stretching out, pillowing us on each other's arms, on true*
> *jewel-arms,*
> *With outstretched legs, oh, will we sleep.*
> *Luxuriant liquor, oh, pray, lift up!"*

The fact that the ancient Japanese patiently bore any amount of pain for conquering love is illustrated in how His Augustness the Deity-of-Eight-Thousand Spears found his Empress, that is Her Augustness the Forward-Princess, and married her; he was put in a snake-house by her angry father when he discovered their love, and again in a house filled with centipedes when he was rescued. And after many happenings His Augustness the Deity-of-Eight-Thousand Spears grasped the hair of the father of the Princess, while he was sleeping, and tied it fast to the various rafters of the house, and after blocking up the floor of the house with a huge rock, he carried off his new wife on his back, and ran away. It is written in the book that when he ran away, the heavenly-speaking lute which he also carried on his back brushed against a tree and the beautiful voice of the lute resounded, shaking the earth. I think that our old ancestors had quite a developed sense of music; here is a story, the most beautiful of all the stories which illustrates their delicacy of feeling.

There was in the reign of the Emperor Nintoku a tall tree on the west bank of the river Tsuki; the shadow of this tree, on its being struck by the morning sun, it is said, reached to the Island of Ahaji, and on being struck by the evening sun, it crossed Mount Takayasu. When the tree was cut down, it was made into a vessel which proved to be a very swift-going one, and it was called by the name of Karanu. With this vessel the water of the Island of Ahaji was drawn morning and evening and presented as the great august water. The vessel became ruined and useless in time; some broken pieces of this old vessel were used as fuel to dry salt, and other pieces of wood that remained over from the burning were turned into a lute, whose sound beautifully re-echoed seven miles away. Some one sang, saying:

> *"Karanu was burned for salt;*
> *The part that was left was made into a lute;*
> *Oh, when, struck, listen, it sounds*
> *Like the wet trees standing*
> *Hocked on the reefs in the middle of the wave,*
> *In the middle of the Yura Sea."*

V

The Poets of Present Japan

I

THE CONSERVATISM OF JAPANESE "POETRY" often proved to be a cowardice with little claim to wisdom; the poets (here I mean chiefly the thirty-one-syllable *Uta* writers) had been taught it was a dignity to rigidly observe the ancient form and spirit. Though I admit that changes are not always a triumph, and that modernity is not an emancipation altogether, their loyalty was more or less a literary superstition. They had to appear at least under a self-denying guise. Uniformity was their special virtue, individuality was regarded by them to be little short of vulgarity. Their poems turned to be the expression of an etiquette whose formality took the place of life and beauty; no sudden change was permitted in their old kingdom. And any conscious introduction of foreign elements, any advance in diction, imagery, or motive, was not readily recognised. The limitation which originated as a test of strength now degenerated to a confession of weakness. There was a time when we thought that nothing could be more perfect than our little poems, and they are remarkable, in fact, but "for what they are not, rather than for what they are," as W. C. Aston cleverly put it; indeed, wonderful in their felicity of phrase, melody of versification, and true sentiment, within their narrow limits. But that was ages ago. The *Uta* poets had been already for a long time a sort of dilettantes who did no small harm to the development of our Japanese poetry, which, under any circumstances, could not be left alone to be ruined. Modern Japan is the age of evolution and expansion; our poetry also began to undergo their influence. It would be more proper, however, to say that the *Uta* poets were left undisturbed with full freedom to stick to the original key if they wanted to, while the younger poets for themselves started a new form of poem called *Shintaishi*, meaning the new-styled poem, with larger scope and greatly increased resources; it is well-nigh reaching already to some achievement.

It is true that the simplicity of our old *Uta* poets was a source of charm and often surprise, and at the same time it was rather tragic for the poets to be forced to keep it up. They were obliged to make a completely unconditional surrender to the ancient form and thought, and to spin from the same old subjects. The changing seasons, the voice of a running stream, the snow-capped Fuji Yama, waves on the beach, the singing of insects or birds, a cherry-blossom, maple-leaves, Spring rains, longing for home, and the like, were the subjects. The *Uta* poets lamented over the dead, and complained enough about the uncertainty of life; but their voices were not from their actual study of real life; they never speculated of Heaven and where they should go after death. Repetition is not without delight entirely when it is musical; but we shall grow very tired of being suggested the same thing all the time; monotony is often suicidal. But our *shintai-shijin* (the new-styled poem-writers) broke off at once from such a prejudice which is, at its best, the refuge of an impoverished mind; and they left the old home of restriction and flew out into the freedom of nature and life. We may say that our Japanese poetry received a baptism; and it seems it has somehow revived.

Not only the subjects, the form of the poetry as well underwent a change. The modern poets could not rest satisfied with the hereditary shape, which consisted of five phrases of lines of 5, 7, 5, 7, and 7 syllables, 31 syllables in all. (And there is another shorter form, consisting of 5, 7, and 5, which you already know in *Hokku*.) To-day they make their own forms to fit their own songs; some use lines of 5 and 7, repeating them to a considerable length as they wish, while some use lines of 7 and 6; many forms like 5 and 5; 7 and 7; 8 and 6; 7 and 8; 7 and 4; 7 and 6; 3, 3, and 4; 4, 7, and 6; 5, 7, and 7; 5, 7, and 5; and others have been invented to advantage. But since every syllable of the Japanese language ends in a vowel, and there are only five vowels, no poet could be successful in the use of rhyme: the result would be only intolerably monotonous if we used it. However, there are many who attempt to overcome the weakness; and even alliteration has been introduced. We have a trick of words in *Uta* poetry called *makura kotoba* or "pillow-words," standing at the beginning of a verse, and serving, as it were, as the pillow upon which it rests; it might be said to be an adjective in many cases; but always it is unintelligible and often absurd. Another bit of word-jugglery is the "pivot-words"; a word or a part of a word is used in two senses; one, with what precedes, the other with what follows. The use of such artifices is utterly despised by our modern poets. The old poets tabooed in their poetry the introduction of a monosyllable

Chinese word, which the *shintai-shijin* freely use; and again the latter are not shy about using even English. Like the English poets, they have begun to use the personification of abstract qualities. In one word, they are not so very different from them in writing lyrics, ballads, allegories, epics, and so forth. However, it may be some time yet before we see real development of the drama. Some ten or fifteen years ago the poems of "storm and stress" overflowed in Japan; in this phase our poets were not far behind their Western brothers.

It was in the early fifteenth of Meiji (1882) when the *Shintaishi* were first introduced by the professors of the Imperial University, the late Masakazu Toyama, Tetsutaro Inouye, and others, who published their collections of new poems and translations from the Western poets. But in fact there was not much to consider till Toson Shimazaki appeared some ten years later.

II

SHIMAZAKI'S *WAKANASHU* ENTHRONED HIM AT once as the master of *Shintaishi*; in that respect he reminds us of Bryant, who suddenly illumined the dearth of early American poetry. (How undeveloped was this new-style poem before his appearance like a comet!) Even Shimazaki's actual work of his early days, *A Ramble in the Forest* for instance, with quite an interesting interruption in a sort of duet:

Mountain Spirit

"The deer, when they fall to death,
Return to love of their wives.

"The fields and hills, when they wither away,
Return to Spring a thousand years old."

Tree Spirit

"Let us bury the old fallen leaves
Under the shadow of leaves, tender, green.

"Awake from winter's dream-road,
Come to this forest of Spring."

might be called a Japanese interpretation of Thanatopsis. We have more than one reason to compare him with Bryant. He began his work at the right time when it was easier for a poet to sing, and at the same time easier for us to listen; it was in the idyllic years, if we may say so (though they passed quickly as anything else in Japan) those four or five years we enjoyed before the China-Japan war which changed abruptly the aspect, atmosphere, and aspiration of the country, vivified the sense of life, and raised the question of the relation of man with man as well as of country with country. It was perfectly natural for Shimazaki to start as a poet of Nature; as I understand, the landscape school of poetry is always first to appear in any country. On reading his poems to-day we cannot help showing our dissatisfaction with his want of persistence and minute observation; and we need more enthusiasm, and some higher poetic dash. But his tone, sentiment, and responsive imaginativeness which were brewed in the time when criticism was not so keen, and the impression of foreign knowledge not so strong as to-day, must be regarded fairly; they give a delightful relief to our minds. In them he has a strong claim. He was a poet of sentiment, almost inclined to be sentimental; he was always delicate, and often sad. (I should like to know where is a Japanese poet who is not sad.) He hated, as any other Japanese poet, the song of wisdom, faith, and liberty; he was flexible in his mind, extremely facile in ear and voice. His voice was that of a youth which has never received any deep scratch from life; and his love, which was passionate enough, but not from real experience, was only a speculation of his dream; and then, the shade and colour of his love were very young, always fresh. He was a poet of Spring, when the flowers commingle with the birds to complete a beautiful concert.

He was not a Tennyson who had a Keats and a Shelley for his predecessors; in one sense, he was an originator. We cannot so severely criticise his diction, which, in fact, cannot be compared with that of a later poet who has boundless vocabularies at his command. He is a poet of a few words; with a few words, he wrote a far better poem than you could expect. And he was not a poet of a few great poems; we must see him as a whole; it is true that he has no wonderful expressions nor separate lines for quotation. However, it is delightful to notice that he could not pretend to a feeling which he did not enjoy, nor did he hunt emotion and rapture for writing's sake as do the later poets. His cadences and pauses were so pleasing. He was meditative, but not slow and also not profound; in one word, he was elementary. And that is one reason why even to-day all the beginners of *Shintaishi* should go to him first; he is the father of the "new-style" poem in that sense. (That is also like Bryant in America.)

In those days Rossetti and Swinburne were not known in Japan, and Wordsworth, Tennyson, and Longfellow were the only names. However, I am not sure at which shrine he burned his incense, although it is clear enough that he was greatly influenced by the Western magic. He who sang the nature and beauty of love in his first book of verses, began to weave the grief and tears of love in his *Ichiyoshu*; here I notice a certain touch of Saigyo Hoshi, that great sad poet of the Kamakura period, whose Oriental longing was deepened by Occidental suggestiveness. He associated nature with the ineffable yearning of art; and he entered into the bosom of silence to seek his own home of poetry and ideal.

> "The light of the moon,
> Shining quiet,
> Why does it make me think
> Incessantly?
> The shadow of the moon
> Has no voice,
>
> But it does steal
> Into one's bosom
> Oh! I who am going to die
> From the world and love!
> My thought which I do not tell,
> And this shadow of the moon,
> Which is more silent?
> Which more sad?"

However, from the oppression of life's meaning, he could not stay young and dreamy, and suddenly stopped singing when he left Tokyo for Shinano, where he became a school-teacher. When he appeared again in literature, it was as a successful novelist. His life as a poet was short, but monumental.

We must come to Bansui Tsuchii to find a representative of the culture and knowledge that advanced in no small degree with the Imperial University as their centre. (By the way, Tsuchii is a University man.) His real qualification as a poet is rather doubtful, but at the same time he is a living proof that a made poet, when he is properly made, is not altogether unacceptable. It is true that he made his Western learning help him to make a better display. It goes without saying that he was never moved by sudden instinct and quickening pulses; but he was glad to scrutinise the phases of Nature, and the universal soul and ideal. He observed wisdom through Hugo and perhaps Schiller (he did not confine his reading to the English poets), and he was pleased to add his own endorsement to them. The admirable part is that his poetical attitude was always sincere, his conception of life grave and just, but without tenderness. He was the first to wrestle with Eternity, and he did not return without something to his profit. His intellectual faculties were very well balanced, almost to the discreetest degree; and under their right guidance he expressed his poetical thought, but that is not to say fire. So his poem was a result, not a first intention, whatever. His deliberation and thought were praiseworthy; ethics was always in his view.

> *"Ané (elder sister) and Imo (younger sister), who were fed*
> *By the same Nature's, the same mother's honourable hands,*
> *The flower of the sky is called Star,*
> *The star of our world ia called Flower.*

> *"This and that are parted afar,*
> *But their odour is the same, Star and Flower,*
> *Laughter and Light they interchange sweet,*
> *Every Eve, Flower and Star.*

> *"But when the clouds of the dawn grow white,*
> *And the flower of the sky fades away,*
> *Do you not see a drop of dew?*
> *The star of our world is crying."*

We notice that many young poets grew nursed by wrong poets, and were carried away by the wild and fantastic passion and fire of a thoughtless youth. But there is no sounder poet than this Tsuchii, whose noble attitude of reverence toward the Western knowledge kept him at the proper place, and even helped him find the right clue of poetical mystery as he wished. Although his individual note was not impressive, his poems prove his clear truimph over that knowledge and culture which did not appear to him as a distraction; and I will say that he was their best harvester. He was wise to desert his fellow university poets of pseudo-classicism like Takejima or Shioi, and he gained a voice sonorous and rhapsodic, though not particularly rich, yet always attractive, from his excursion into the Chinese diction. Shimazaki was frequently effeminate, but Tsuchii was manly. He was always correct, and comprehensive, so then he lacked a touch of illusion. I am ready to say that he was quite commonplace, but he succeeded in making his commonplaceness often suggestive. I believe that it is no small art.

Those who wished for a deeper colour and variety of diction than Shimazaki's, and showed a fatigue at his monotony, open their arms to welcome Kyukin Susukida. Susukida enshrined Keats in his heart; like him he is a poet of Youth and Beauty, to whom Nature appeared as a background. At least so he was in his earlier books, *Yukuharu* and *Botekishu*. I do not say that he did not understand Nature, but he did not attempt to see her with his naked eyes, and he tried to robe her with his own idealistic robes. He did not incline to solve Nature and Life as Tsuchii, but he made them a symbol of love and poetry, through which he looked for salvation. He was a dreamer, but he never speculated in thought. He was simple. He hated the world vulgar and material. He is a poet of unerring culture who built the house beautiful, which he peopled with his choicest images and longing, who put beauty and melody of language before everything else. He has been verily often criticised as a classicist. It is true that his taste was refined by virtue of his training, and he could be quite graceful even when he had nothing to say. On the other hand, his mind never rose high, he brought no particular message to our life. His chief merit must be valued through the channel of his language which gives us a delightful change from Shimazaki; indeed, he is the master of art, he had no competitor in its beauty. However, in his later work, there is plenty of reason to believe that he was trying to escape from his culture and classicism which benefited him at the beginning; it is almost tragic to see his struggle. His hands are too delicate after a long habit of wearing gloves; he is not accustomed so well to the open air. His views of life and beauty are far more advanced in his *Nijugogen* and *Hakuyokyu* than in his earlier books; but it seems that he could not leave his classicism entirely. If he were smaller or larger than himself, I should say that he would be better off; his strength is, after all, his weakness.

We have two other interesting poets of modern Japan in Ariake Kanbara and Homei Iwano.

III

It seems to me that Ariake Kanbara had been wandering in the labyrinth of experiment (how he loved that wandering), not knowing exactly where he would come out; he has much enthusiasm; his sensitive mind made his poetical ambition quick to flame up over a new thing. His travelling guide or companion was Rossetti at first, when he strove to hold the vision and romance of his own kingdom of music and love, his eternal land of imagination and youth:

> *"I stand alone, and I hear*
> *The whisper sad,—*
> *'Tis Heaven's whisper over the far-away sea,*
> *Which the white sunbeams spoke.*

> *"The voice is lone but clear,*
> *Quiet but bright,*
> *I can never know the whisper of the far-away sea,*
> *The whisper of the shining sky."*

I have been thinking sometimes that he had a false start in his poetical work; it is true that he needed somebody to support him when he could not walk by himself; but even at the time when he was perfectly able to manage himself, his face still turned instinctively toward his original help. We read many reflections and echoes of Rossetti even in his latest work. (By the way, he is the author of some four books of poems, the latest being *Ariake Shu*.) To have a support at the start is nothing particularly bad; but at the same time it is enough of a disadvantage. It is a question of genuineness for poetry; realisation is the main thing.

He has been often charged with vagueness; I should say that he has only to smile over such a charge. We are rather glad that he has no aim of amusing his readers in fact, there he shows a poet's dignity. Vagueness is often a virtue; a god lives in a cloud; truth cannot be put on one's finger-tip. The darkness of night is beauty; that is only another view of the light of day. Still we know that when a poet is great, he always goes back to the simplicity of nature; there may come a time for him when he will cry for that simplicity as a child for his mother's milk. In fact, when he returned to simplicity he was most delightful, as in the case of Browning; read one of his poems called "Shu no Madara" or "The Dark Red Shadow-Spots" with the following lines somewhere:

> *"Between the spaces,*
> *Of acacia branches commingled,*
> *Spread on*
> *The shining crown of clouds.*
>
> *Two alone in the shadowy lane,*
> *You and I;*
> *Oh how lovely,*
> *The fragrance of the green!*
>
> *"The breezes fan,*
> *The leaves of the acacia trees*
> *Turn on*
> *Dreamily.*
>
> *"The dark-red shadow-spots of the sun*
> *Swing;*
> *Alas, of a sudden,*
> *My thought disordered."*

He is a builder of a brick house who sets his materials with care; he is a curio-shop keeper who arranges his bric-a-brac with no small taste. He is not a free bird who sings to a star; but he is a caged nightingale who sings beautifully. His understanding of what it is to be a poet is thorough; and he can be that quite easily. However, his poetical atmosphere is rather close and shut up; his mind is too systematic; he has too good a head to be a great poet. What is symbolism if not "the affirmation of your own temperament in other things, the spinning of a strange thread which will bind you and the other phenomena together"? Kanbara is that symbolist; he looks upon everything with his own special personality. We have no symbols in the strict literary meaning; it seems to me that he has a great chance before him; and if he can work out his own symbolism, he may create a special cult for the future generation to follow. But we are rather doubtful of the nature of his faith; I have some reason to think that his symbolism may be only a fancy, that it has no root in the ground. It may be his love, but not a purpose; and that is a weak point for him. He has elaborate adjectives, phrases, and description, but we are sure he must find some other way to make his poem alive. Truth and beauty want no explanation, nor pomp of line. His poetical mind is clear like a looking-glass which reflects every line and colour. But his enemy is himself; he has too much restraint, a certain heaviness, unmistakable difficulty with his lines, appeals too much to the reader's eye; he has an excess of exactitude which only makes him difficult to follow. He uses too often a sharpened pencil to make a landscape of large size; it makes the picture a failure as a whole; he spoils the general effect by paying too diligent attention to details. He is a wonder of development; he is a poet of taste. He takes a little seed of a strange flower, puts it in the ground, waters it, makes it bloom, places it on a tokonoma, and gazes at and admires it from every side; he does not require a great subject to sing on. But his poetical mood is often sophisticated; he is too careful, too timid, like a shy bird. And if he grasps life's meaning, unfortunately he kills it. It would be his triumph if he could leave out his classicism which he himself created. He has to conquer his own soul; he has to learn the emotion of faith which is primal After all, his cleverness would be only his own fault. Some critic said that Mallarmé (Kanbara's art, which originated in Rossetti, was improved later by Mallarmé and other French poets) was obscure, not so much because he wrote differently, but because he thought differently, from other people; now I should like to say the same thing of Kanbara. He thinks with a strange thought; how many people of Japan could understand Rossetti or Mallarmé? There are so many echoes of them in Kanbara's poems; but I do not mean to underestimate his worth; in that shade he is worthy and even wonderful.

IV

I HAVE MUCH TO SAY on Homei Iwano. We hear of a poet of promise with youthfulness and a certain amateurish fire, but never reaching to a state of maturity; such a poet is rarely guilty of falsehood or artificiality, but his want of the power of self-analysis is often wonderful. Iwano is one of that class.

"'Tis too sweet—ah, the joy of the world,
Spring joins with the road of dream; what a vision
(Light mist afar, sleeping flowers anear)
Goes round my spirit's eyes.

"Let me bid my careless love adieu,
Under the window the slender rains fall on;
My yearning of the springing passion
Would live in the breeze under the cloudy sky."

His poem is that of mood, whether of love or other emotion; and we are often sad when we are disenchanted, the veil of his muse's shrine having fallen. He is a too open singer; his voice sometimes drops even into bathos. Suggestion, the spirit of atmosphere should be properly valued; and we do not attempt to hold back the poet when he flies into the clouds. Iwano's imagination shows great variety in wealth and colour without depth, like a summer cloud which haunts the mountain peak. Questions in philosophy and reflection are not his own field; but his speculation in thought and passion makes one of ten wonder and gaze. His poems themselves are his personality. His is the poetry of his transition age; will he ever reach the time of realisation? Doubtless his spiritual life will evolve and he will gain intimacy with Nature in time. I think, however, that poetical sureness is more often born than made. It is a pity that he is much troubled with the richness of his own fire and thought, and, in spite of himself, loses his self-consciousness. We cannot find the silence and the odour of time and association in his free and often undisciplined songs. His head never turns back to the twilight, but looks forward to the sunrise and the sky. He has been accused of being an unthinking singer, who scatters his thoughts and wastes his passion on any subject; in fact, he is at home on any subject, his sudden fire and thought rising up on the spot. He is the most versatile poet of the present day; and, naturally, he has unconsciously degenerated into every excess. And it seems to me that he always lacks just one touch of distinction. The heart of Nature is sad. Beyond the sounds of the wind and the waves you will be impressed by the loneliness and beauty of silence, which is the dignity of Nature. The real poem should be like it. But it is regrettable in Iwano that his voice often stops at being only a voice, and lacks something which should lie beyond. On the other hand, his buoyancy and exaltation of imagination and swing are the outburst of his own nature, frequently reminding us of the Celtic. (He is the Irish singer of Japan.) The question with him is not how to sing, but how not to sing. He was a poet ardently following after a romantic colour in life and passion when he published his *Homei Shishu*. I noticed then that his romanticism, too, tottered toward a sad confusion. But I begin to observe a great change in his later work. He is a born poet, and in any circumstances can be trusted as to his genuineness. He is not a bric-a-brac poet whatever, but has yet to learn how to control his poetic impulse, which is his only guide. His mood is so compelling that he is carried on by the force of momentum, and troubled with his own gift. While I know that the gospel of the negative cannot be admired, some sense of limitation would do him a world of good. He wrote "Tankyoku" in the *Sad Love and Sad Song*, the fourteen-line songs which proved successful. They are impressive in their own special way, one dwelling on a speculation in thought, and another carrying a terribly realistic picture of passion. What he sings in them is less Japanese than universal. "Tankyoku" is not a sonnet which should be rigid in form and idea; it is simply written in fourteen lines:

> *"Holding a stone which has no voice,*
> *I cry my world away with tears;*
> *'Tis not for love as the other people say,*
> *'Tis not for the pain which I suffer most,*
> *'Tis more than my pain and love;*
> *My flesh of burning thoughts will burn,*
> *And my hot tears alone run down,*
> *When the loneliness in my bosom comes to flow.*
> *Nor God nor Death is in me;*
> *If there is a thing, 'tis this loneliness:*
> *Now I am a prey of my own life,*
> *And cry away this endless world with the stone;*
> *It bears silence eternally growing,*
> *And I pour on it my own tears."*

It is acknowledged that in his later work he has deserted the golden realm of romanticism and entered delightfully into the silver-grey cloud-land of symbolism; and he has made a better friendship with Verlaine, and taken him as a bosom friend without any proper etiquette, and even thinks that he is himself a Japanese Verlaine. I am sure that there is no slightest harm in it. I do not call his transformation to some sort of symbolism from romanticism an advance to a higher poetical plane—it is simply his line of evolution. And I see a delightful change in Iwano of to-day. But somehow I suspect that in his idea and poetry he is lusting after strange gods and kneeling to them in too free adoration. I even declare that he offends sometimes, but without any bad intention against good taste and discretion; and I espy that he appears quite glad in his own action. It is not a rebellion in his case by any means, but a revolution. But what is the saddest thing with this Iwano is that he has lately stopped singing; he is squandering his own talent and passion on novel-writing and criticism. It is not alone myself that wishes his return to poetry.

There are other names who have helped to make this new-styled poems or *Shintaishi* a strong literary force and brought it to the present development—for instance, Hakusei Hiraki, who grasps a large subject and executes with a rigid construction and handsome but passionless rhetoric; Tetsukan Yosano, whose life-long training in *Uta*-writing made his poems terse, and whose experience of life flashes sharp; Suimei Kawai, whose calm rhythm and tender beauty of feeling might suggest a Longfellow; Kagai Kodama, whose Byronic fire and surprise cannot be overlooked; and Gekko Takayasu, who is the singer of Kyoto, the old capital, where he lives, that is to say, an appreciator of quieter life and somewhat old but pleasing ideality. And lastly, we cannot forget the name of Tokoku Kitamura, a singer of Byronism, who, some years before Shimazaki, already breathed a new poetical spirit into the poetry of modern Japan; in truth, he might be termed the father of *Shintaishi*. The development of the last few years brought to the front two names, Hakushu Kitahara and Rofu Miki, to whose work special attention should be called.

VI

SOME UTA SPECIMENS FROM THE HYAKUNIN ISHIU ANTHOLOGY COMPILED IN 1235 BY SADAIYE, A NOBLE OF THE KYOTO COURT

"The flowers and my love
Passed away under the rain,
While I idly looked upon them
Where is my yester-love?"

—ONO NO KOMACHI

O no no Komachi," Ki no Tsurayuki remarks, "belongs to the school of Sotoori Hime of ancient times. There is feeling in her poems, but little vigour. She is like a lovely woman who is suffering from ill health. Want of vigour, however, is only natural in a woman's poetry." Although she left little work, her poetical capacity as well as her beauty, it is said, caused her to be called to the Imperial House. She was not from a family of high position by any means, as she was a daughter of a certain chief officer of a county. There is no other woman of old Japan whose life figures so largely in fiction; and her name as a model of beauty more than as a poetess is universally known. Komachi is regarded as a synonym of "beautiful woman"; there were or are many beautiful women nicknamed Komachi. Whether a fiction or not, Fukakusa no Chujo's love-story with her is famous: it is said that his love was utterly scorned, and he called her to admit him to her house with no success whatever, and that he died under the winter snow on his hundredth journey.

"Behold the heavenly vastness,
The sky of the moon!
Is it not the same moon I once saw
Out of Kasuga's Mikasa hill?"

—ABE NO NAKAMARO

Abe no Nakamaro left Japan for China in his sixteenth year, and stayed in China for thirty-eight long years. The Emperor Benso admired his ability and appointed him as his secretary; and Nakamaro changed his name and took the Chinese name of Choko, and considered himself as a Chinese. But it was the 4th of Tenbio Shoho (729), when the Japanese ambassador to China, Fujiwara no Kiyokawa, was going back, and Nakamaro's thought of home stirred. And he decided to return to Japan; and many of his friends, Oi and Rihaku, the two famous Chinese poets, among them, held a farewell party in Nakamaro's honour. It was a moonlit night when the dinner took place, and he wrote this *Uta* thinking about the moon that used to come out of Kasuga's Mikasa hill, which he knew well in his boyhood days. The Mikasa hill is in the outskirts of Nara. It is said that every member of the party wept over his *Uta*. However, Nakamaro could not return home after all; the ship in which he sailed met with a tempest, and he was shipwrecked. He died in China at the age of eighty-one.

> *"O thou, fisher's boat,*
> *Tell men that I sailed*
> *Away into the eighty isles,*
> *Into the bluest field, the sea!"*

—SANGI TAKAMURA

This Sangi Takamura's *Uta* was written when he was put in a boat to be an exile in the far-away Iki island. It happened that he had been appointed vice-ambassador to China, the chief being Fujiwara no Tsunetsuyu, and the four ships which were to take the entire company were announced officially. And the first ship which Tsunetsuyu rode in was damaged when it had hardly left the shore, and he insisted on having Takamura exchange ships for his safety. The latter grew angry, and at once turned the head of his boat and landed; and he resigned, saying that his old father needed him so that he could not go so far off. The Emperor Saga (810–842) was obliged to impose on him an official punishment since he had disobeyed his august command for such a reason.

He wrote some seventy *Uta* poems on his exile journey, which are said to be beautiful in diction and full of meaning. This *Uta* is one of them.

"To gaze upon the moon
Is to be sad in a thousand ways,
Though all the Autumn
Is not meant to be my own self's."

—OYE NO CHIZATO

"'Tis the Spring day
With lovely far-away light.
Why must the flowers fall
With hearts unquiet?"

—KI NO TOMONORI

Some commentator says that this *Uta* poem is the best among all the *Uta* poems ever written in Japan.

"Alas, my face betrayed
The secret of my love.
All men ask me why
I am so sad."

—TAIEA NO KANEMOEI

"That I love thee
Is known already. Ah, me!
I had been thinking that
No one would know it."

—MIBU NO TADAMI

This *Uta* was written, it is said, on the 2nd of Tentoku (957), when the Emperor Reizei gathered the court poets and poetesses to hold an *Uta* contest. Among the love poems on this occasion, this is one of the best, the other best one being Taira no Kanemori's *Uta*, which precedes this poem. The poetical umpire Ononomiya pronounced Kanemori's the better. Tadami took the failure too hard to his heart; and it is said that he died after ceasing to eat for some days.

"The moon has nothing to make
Me think and cry,

But, alas, my own tears alone
    Do lament and fall."

—SAIGYO HOSHI

"Oh, thread of my life,
Be torn off now if it must!
I fear in longer life
My secret would be hard to keep."

—SHIKISHI NAISHINNO

"I might show thee
How the Oshima island fishers' sleeves
Never change their tints, though wet through.
But, alas, tearful sleeves of mine!"

—IMPUKU MONIN NO OSUKE

"List, the crickets sing!
Upon the mat of the frost-night,
I, my raiment not yet unbound,
    Have to sleep alone."

—GOKYOKOKU SESSHO SAKINO DAJODAIJIN

"'Tis not the stormy snow
Luring the garden flower,
But what is falling fast
Is nothing but my own self."

—NYUDO SAKINO DAJODAIJIN

"My sleeves are like
The wide sea rocks unseen
Even at the lowest tide. Nobody would know
That their tears never dry."

—NIJONOIN SANUKI

Some *Hokku* Specimens by the Masters

"To-day, at last to-day,
I grew to wish to raise
The chrysanthemum flowers."

—Ransetsu

"Autumn's full moon;
Lo, the shadows of a pine tree
Upon the mats!"

—Kikaku

"Yellow chrysanthemum, white chrysanthemum:
Why, the other names for me
Are of no use."

—Ransetsu

"'Let day pass,
Let night break.'
The frogs sing—they sing morning and eve."

—Buson

"Ah, how sublime—
The green leaves, the young leaves,
In the light of the sun!"

—Basho

A Note About the Author

Yone Noguchi (1875–1947) was a Japanese poet, novelist, and critic who wrote in both English and Japanese. Born in Tsushima, he studied the works of Thomas Carlyle and Herbert Spencer at Keio University in Tokyo, where he also practiced Zen and wrote haiku. In 1893, he moved to San Francisco and began working at a newspaper established by Japanese exiles. Under the tutelage of Joaquin Miller, an Oakland-based writer and outdoorsman, Noguchi came into his own as a poet. He published two collections in 1897 before moving to New York via Chicago. In 1901, he published *The American Diary of a Japanese Girl*, his debut novel. Noguchi soon tired of America, however, and sailed to England where he published a third book of poems and made connections with such writers as William Butler Yeats and Thomas Hardy. Reinvigorated and determined to continue his career, he returned to New York in 1903, but left for Japan the following year following the end of his marriage to journalist and educator Léonie Gilmour, with whom he had a son. As the Russo-Japanese War brought his nation onto the world stage, Noguchi became known as a literary critic for the *Japan Times* and focused on advising such Western playwrights as Yeats to study the classical Noh drama. He spent the second decade of the century as a prominent international lecturer, mainly in Europe and Britain. In 1920, Noguchi published *Japanese Hokkus*, a collection of short poems, before turning his attention to Japanese-language verse. As Japan moved closer toward war with the West, Noguchi turned from leftist politics to the nationalism supported by his country's leaders, straining his relationship with Bengali poet Rabindranath Tagore and distancing himself from his former colleagues around the world. In 1945, his home in Tokyo was destroyed in the devastating American firebombing of the city; he died only two years later, having reconnected with his son Isamu.

A Note from the Publisher

Spanning many genres, from non-fiction essays to literature classics to children's books and lyric poetry, Mint Edition books showcase the master works of our time in a modern new package. The text is freshly typeset, is clean and easy to read, and features a new note about the author in each volume. Many books also include exclusive new introductory material. Every book boasts a striking new cover, which makes it as appropriate for collecting as it is for gift giving. Mint Edition books are only printed when a reader orders them, so natural resources are not wasted. We're proud that our books are never manufactured in excess and exist only in the exact quantity they need to be read and enjoyed.

Discover more of your favorite classics with Bookfinity™.

- Track your reading with custom book lists.
- Get great book recommendations for your personalized Reader Type.
- Add reviews for your favorite books.
- AND MUCH MORE!

Visit **bookfinity.com** and take the fun Reader Type quiz to get started.

Enjoy our classic and modern companion pairings!

Books by Deborah Aubrey-Peyron

Miraculous Interventions™ Series *:

Miraculous Interventions™

MI-II *Modern Day Priests, Prophets, Pastors & Everyday Visionaries*

MI-III *2012 The Miraculous Year*

MI-IV *The Gathering Season*

The Sampler of Miraculous Interventions   *[Bks 1 – 4]*

MI-V *The Small, Still Voice*

MI-VI *The Warning*

MI-VII *The Saving of America*

MI-VIII *Extraordinary Miracles*

Best of Miraculous Interventions™ Series *[Bks 1-4]*

Best of Miraculous Interventions™ Books V - VIII

Sampler of Miraculous Interventions™ Series, I - VIII

Christmas Chaos!

Christmas Chaos! Coloring book

An Old Man's Christmas (*by Ronald J. Aubrey and Deborah Aubrey-Peyron)*

Deb's Christmas Cookbook, *Four Generations of Family Recipes*

Let's Take a Walk, Dave, *The David Becker Story*

You Are My Sunshine (*Co-written with Lisa Wisdom)*

My Story, *Richard Riddell Mosely*

My Faith Journey, *Dennis Murphy, Miracles I Have Experienced*

[*Miraculous Interventions™ is abbreviated, "MI" in this list]

The stories in these books have been written in order to encourage the brethren and inspire the secular world.